Tatting

Rhoda L. Auld

Tatting

the contemporary art of knotting with a shuttle

Drawings by James Wood

Photographs by Lawrence Auld

VNR VAN NOSTRAND REINHOLD COMPANY

NEW YORK CINCINNATI TORONTO LONDON MELBOURNE

To Warren and Vivian, who, while thi...
being written, tended to regard it with mix...
if it were a new baby in the family

Frontispiece
Tatted panel by Rhoda Auld. Flower motifs, figure of girl,
and mesh ground are tatted, bodice is crocheted.

The author and Van Nostrand Reinhold Company have
taken all possible care to trace the ownership of every
work of art reproduced in this book and to make full ac-
knowledgment for its use. If any errors have accidentally
occurred, they will be corrected in subsequent editions,
provided notification is sent to the publisher.

Designed by Donald E. Munson
Photographs by Lawrence Auld except for museum-owned
pieces other than those from Horner Museum and Lincoln County
Historical Museum

First published in paperback in 1981
Copyright © 1974 by Rhoda L. Auld
Library of Congress Catalog Card Number 73-14011
ISBN 0-442-20416-7

Van Nostrand Reinhold Company Inc.
135 West 50th Street, New York, NY 10020

Fleet Publishers
1410 Birchmount Road, Scarborough, Ontario M1P 2E7

Van Nostrand Reinhold Australia Pty. Ltd.
480 Latrobe Street, Melbourne, Victoria 3000, Australia

Van Nostrand Reinhold Company Ltd.
Molly Millars Lane, Wokingham, Berkshire, England RG11 2PY
Cloth edition published 1974 by Van Nostrand Reinhold Company
16 15 14 13 12 11 10 9 8 7 6 5 4 3

Library of Congress Cataloging in Publication Data

Auld, Rhoda L.
  Tatting.

  Bibliography: p.
  1. Tatting. I. Title
TT840.A87   746.4'3   73-14011
ISBN 0-442-20416-7

Acknowledgments

I should like to thank those who took time to answer inquiries,
especially the members of the International Old Lacers whom
I canvassed heavily; those who permitted us to photograph
their own work or tatting from their collections; those who
loaned books, tatting and tatting tools; and those who contri-
buted ideas.

Special thanks to those who donated objects to my own
collection, including Gerry Koss who sent me a bracelet to
which shortened crochet hooks can be attached, and particularly to Sadie G. Allison for her five-inch shuttle, which I
treasure; to Elizabeth Solmon, who gave up a morning to
pose for pictures; and to St. Mary's Academy, Portland, and
Sister Ann Harold who allowed us to copy the section on
tatting in Mrs. Pullan's book.

I am most deeply indebted to Susan E. Munstedt who has
long been teaching tatting with a length of twine rather than
with a shuttle. She also suggested immersing tatted motifs in
dipping plastic, and I appreciate her willingness to share
these and other ideas.

I am obliged to Mary J. Buchanan of the Corvallis Public
Library for ordering many books from the Oregon State Li-
brary, and to Miriam Minnick, Interlibrary Loan Librarian at
Oregon State University.

I have quoted or used patterns from the following: *The
Works of the English Poets, from Chaucer to Cowper
. . .* (London: Printed for J. Johnson et al., 1810), vol. 8; *The
Poetical and Dramatic Works of Sir Charles Sedley*, col-
lected and edited . . . by V. de Sola Pinto (London: Consta-
ble, 1928); *The Spectator,* edited . . . by Donald F. Bond (Ox-
ford: Clarendon Press, 1965), vol 4; *The Autobiography and
Correspondence of Mary Granville, Mrs. Delany . . . ,* edited
by . . . Lady Llanover, 6 vols., i.e., [1st and] 2nd ser. (London:
Richard Bentley, 1861–2); Clara Morris *Life on Stage: My
Personal Experiences and Recollections* (New York:
McClure, Phillips, 1901); Mrs. [Matilda Chesney] Pullan, *The
Lady's Manual of Fancy-Work . . .* (New York: Dick & Fitz-
gerald, 1858); *Peterson's Magazine* (March 1857); Gun
Blomqvist and Elwy Persson, *Frivoliteter* (Stockholm: LTs

Preface

Förlag, 1967); *Collingbourne's New Easy Way of Making Tatting and Maltese Art,* edited by Virginia Snow Studios (Elgin, Ill.: Collingbourne Mills, 1917), book 11.

My authority for word origins was *The Oxford English Dictionary.* I have also depended on information found in the books cited in the bibliography, and in the following: The Oxford Book of Seventeenth Century Verse, chosen by H. J. C. Grierson and G. Bullough (Oxford: Claredon Press, 1934); the chapters by Donald King in *The Connoisseur Period Guides* (London : *Connoisseur,* 1957), vol. 2, *The Stuart Period, 1603-1714*, and vol. 3, *The Early Georgian Period, 1714–1760*; Barbara Snook, *English Historical Embroidery* (London: Batsford, 1960); M. Jordain, *The History of English Secular Embroidery* (London: Kegan Paul, 1910); Boswell's *Life of Johnson . . .* , edited by George Birkbeck Hill. Rev. and enl. ed. by L. F. Powell (Oxford: Clarendon Press, 1934), vol. 4; Gertrude Whiting, *Tools and Toys of Stitchery* (New York: Columbia University Press, 1928); *Mrs. Delany at Court and Among the Wits . . . , arr. from "The Autobiography and Correspondence of Mrs. Delany..."*, with an introd. by R. Brimley Johnson (London: Stanley Paul, 1925); *The Diary of a Country Parson: The Reverend James Woodforde, 1758–1781*, edited by John Beresford (London: Oxford University Press, 1924) [vol. 1]; Georgiana Brown Harbeson, *American Needlework . . .* (New York: Bonanza Books, 1938); S. F. A. Caulfeild and Blanche C. Saward, *The Dictionary of Needlework . . .* , 2d ed. (London: Gill, n.d.); and many, many nineteenth and twentieth-century pattern books. Unfortunately, only broken sets of *Godey's* and *Peterson's* were available to me, and I had no access at all to any of the Frank Leslie publications where I have reason to believe that there is much on tatting.

The idea of reversing the bearing thread for the entire knot rather than just its parts is something I read before this book was conceived. I have been unable to relocate the source, and I regret that I cannot give proper credit. I am grateful to all of the above for their help.

In many communities in the United States and Britain there are people who tat, but most of them are elderly. They prefer to work in the traditional manner, using fine, white crochet cotton to reproduce the lacy edgings and doilies of a past era. Few of them make new designs even within the framework of the old concept. To state this is not to criticize them. They are people who, almost without exception, are generous in their willingness to teach the art to any of the young who see them at it, and who are perceptive enough to realize that something interesting is going on.

Only a small selection of tatting tools is now available, and those are unsuited for the heavy materials used in contemporary handmade textiles. However, equipment for these new materials can be improvised easily and cheaply, and will perform the same functions as the tatting shuttle, which does only two things: it provides a practical way to manage the thread, and it makes it easy to work very fast. With practice, it becomes possible to work quite rapidly and efficiently with improvised tools, too. Teachers, especially, will be glad to know that all the rudiments can be taught using only cotton parcel-post twine and round wooden toothpicks.

A wide range of handsome openwork cloth, adaptable to modern needs, can be produced with new tools. Pillow covers, belts, necklaces, bags, wall hangings, and three-dimensional shapes can all be made, and there are many ways to introduce beads. Combining tatting with other methods like crochet or hairpin lace widens the possibilities of the contemporary technique even further. Combined with stitchery, new forms of tatting echo the craft as it was practiced in the eighteenth century, when, as knotting, it was essentially a kind of embroidery.

Tatting can be simple enough for the most casual hobbyist, yet the serious craftsman will quickly recognize that the art is in its infancy, and offers significant potential for innovation. Although tatting has been traditionally thought of as decoration for other fabrics, especially as a form of lace, there are other ways to think about it and other ways to use it.

It is the purpose of this book to show that tatting has a future as well as a past.

Corvallis, Oregon
August, 1973

Tatted border, with needlepoint-lace centers in the individual circles, made in Ardee, Ireland, about 1880. (Courtesy of the Victoria and Albert Museum. Crown copyright.)

Contents

Woman wearing tatted neckpiece, about 1900.

(Courtesy of Edith M. Hughes.)

Figure 1-1. A star-shaped design made by Elizabeth Harpole Bayley, an Oregon pioneer who died in 1911. (Courtesy of Lincoln County Historical Museum, Newport, Oregon.)

1 / History

The delicate, snowflake-like patterns of tatted lace are familiar to most of us, even if we do not know how to make them. All but the very young have watched the traditional shuttle flit through someone's fingers to produce doilies, or, more likely, trimmings that would later decorate pillowcases, handkerchiefs, clothing, and other items. No matter how complex its structure appears, all tatting, including the contemporary openwork fabrics presented later in this book, is created by repeating a single knot. In fact, the art evolved from the practice of embroidering cloth with closely knotted threads.

Only gradually did tatting develop into more than just a device for decorating other fabrics, and after it emerged from the earliest stage, it remained for a long time only as a means of making edgings and trimmings. Not until the nineteenth century, when people began to invent tatted doilies, collars, and caps, did tatting itself become a way of making fabric. In its short history as a full-fledged textile art, it has been conceived of and used only as lace. In fact, many of its forms were consciously devised in imitation of various traditional lace patterns.

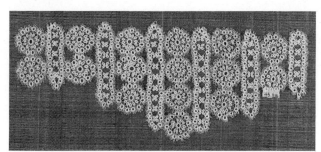

Figure 1-2. Baby dolls dressed in white muslin edged with tatting, about 1900. (Courtesy of Horner Museum, Oregon State University.)

Figure 1-3. After generally serving as edging, tatting became a way of making fabric. Cuff by Elizabeth Bachelder of Andover, New Hampshire, around 1860—70. (Courtesy of Museum of Fine Arts, Boston.)

9

Knotting

Tatting evolved from a particular kind of embroidery, now obscure, but extremely popular throughout Europe in the eighteenth century. With a shuttle, knots were tied at close intervals in thread or cord. The "strings of knots" thus produced, when sewn onto fabric backgrounds in elaborate patterns, resulted in highly decorative cloth.

This kind of needlework was known in England as early as the fifteenth century. However, when it suddenly became all the rage there in the 1690s among the ladies at court, the new popularity did not stem from the native tradition, but was rather a direct result of the opening of the Far East by the Dutch. Evidently, examples of the method, which the Chinese used extensively, were much admired in Holland, and emigrated from there to England with Mary II. Seventeenth-century knotting, then, was an early manifestation of the vogue for chinoiserie, which would later intensify and revolutionize western European styles.

Only a few of the embroideries made by knotting in the seventeenth and eighteenth centuries have survived, but contemporary references to the craft are abundant, beginning with comments in poems by some of William and Mary's courtiers. One by Charles Sackville, Earl of Dorset, tells us that a lady who "sat knotting in a shade" was using an "ivory needle" (a shuttle or possibly a netting needle) and a "twisted ball."

Other references bear witness to the extraordinary popularity of the pastime among the ladies. They include a song by Sir Charles Sedley often called "Phillis Knotting," which was set to music by Sir Henry Purcell. A mild lampoon called "The Royal Knotter," which is also attributed to Sedley, clearly alludes to Queen Mary herself, and lauds her, staunch Protestant that she is, for "knotting Threads" when she rides in her coach instead of "telling Beads" like her Catholic predecessors.

Many eighteenth-century ladies sat for their portraits shuttle in hand. They included Queen Charlotte, wife of George III of England, Mme. Adélaide, daughter of Louis XV of France, and the princess Kunigunde, daughter of the Elector of Saxony. Although the work these ladies are doing does not at first appear to be anywhere in sight, usually, if one looks closely, the knots can be found, even in reduced reproductions, between the left hand and the knotting-bag that almost always hangs from the left wrist. The ornate shuttles of the period were large and wide open at the tips, so that they might accommodate heavy cords.

Figure 1-4. One of a set of yellow silk chairs decorated with red knotted thread, Surrey, England, end of the Stuart period. This shows the early use of knotted lines to produce formal patterns. (Courtesy of the Victoria and Albert Museum. Crown copyright.)

Figure 1-5. Detail of English bed valance, 12 inches wide, first half of eighteenth century. Natural-color linen threads of various weights are couched down to a natural linen ground and accented with satin stitch. This freer style is typical of the early Georgian period. Oriental influence is evident; the design is believed to have been adapted from Chinese wallpaper. (Courtesy of Colonial Williamsburg Collection. Photograph by Delmore A. Wenzel.)

Figure 1-6. Princess Kunigunde with her knotting bag and shuttle, by P. Rotari, 1742. This study of the daughter of the Elector of Saxony may be one of the earliest portraits of a lady knotting. The portion of the cord that runs from the left hand into the bag is closely knotted. (Courtesy Gemäldgalerie, Dresden. Reproduced from the collections of the Library of Congress.)

Figure 1-7. *Portrait de Mme. Danger*, by Louis Tocqué, eighteenth century. So obscure was the art of knotting at the opening of the twentieth century that an English needlework authority mistook the activity, which is clearly knotting, for *parfilage*, the unraveling of gold and silver thread in order to sell it. (Courtesy of the Louvre, Paris.)

Unlike other forms of needlework, knotting was considered a suitable activity for mixed gatherings. In France, especially, it provided the aristocratic lady with an opportunity to show off her elaborate and expensive shuttle wound with costly thread. She flirted with it as she would with a fan, and certainly all this conspicuous show was more important than the relatively little knotting that may have been accomplished. A gentleman might even borrow a shuttle from milady and try his hand at it. Boswell reports Dr. Johnson as saying that he attempted the skill, but failed to learn it. Knotting-bags went everywhere, and one story tells of a shuttle lost by Mme. de Pompadour at the Comédie-Française.

On some occasions, the knotting-bags were not welcome. The *Examiner* for April 24, 1713 bears the following:

Lady *Char___te* is taken *Knotting* in St. *James's Chapel,* during Service, in the immediate Presence both of *God* and *Her Majesty,* who were affronted together.

Figure 1-8. Detail of the same portrait, clearly showing the knots on the thread.

The Transition from Knotting to Tatting

During the Stuart period, knotted thread was used like braid to make formal patterns such as that in Figure 1-4. In the eighteenth century, it was used more freely to make outlines and fillings for large shapes (see fig. 1-5). Although this type of knotting was often monochromatic, usually white on white, various weights of thread and kinds of knot provided textural differences within the design.

A photograph taken in the nineteenth century provides us with an important clue as to how knotting became tatting. Recently discovered and reproduced in *Antiques* (July, 1969), it shows one of a pair of blue chair covers made in 1750 by Mary Granville Delany, which "are bordered with a beautiful pattern . . . of oak leaves cut out in white linen and tacked down with different sorts of white knotting, which forms the veining and stalks." There we see that one row of Mrs. Delany's couched, knotted threads undoubtedly consists of tatted rings.

Mention of what appears to be a pair of shuttles in 1781 in England also gives us a clue as to when tatting became more free standing. Since many tatting patterns use two shuttles, earlier forms may have advanced to tatting by that time, although it is unlikely that anything more elaborate than trimmings were being made. Knotting had by no means died out, however. Nevertheless, no form of the word *tatting* appears in English literature before 1842, though we can safely assume that it was used in the spoken language somewhat before that time. Despite many conjectures about its derivation, the word *tatting* is of unknown origin, and may very well have been invented at someone's whim or caprice. In France, on the other hand, one word, *frivolité*, is used for both knotting and tatting. Tatting is so widespread in Europe, including Turkey, that it is difficult to say whether all of it followed the path from China to the Netherlands, from where it fanned out to the rest of Europe. Perhaps it reached the more easterly areas by an entirely different route.

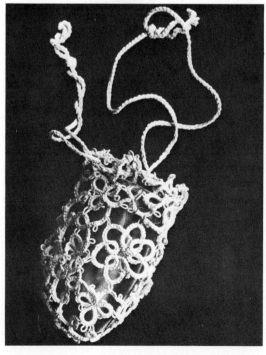

Figure 1-10. Tatted bags, shaped like the traditional bag for holding knotting or tatting equipment, have a long history. In America, around the turn of the century, little girls often carried Sunday school purses just large enough to hold a coin or two. This one from 1915 is lined with red silk. (Courtesy of Edith M. Hughes.)

13

Figure 1-11. Tatted edging, 9½ x 1 inches, German, nineteenth century. (Courtesy of the Metropolitan Museum of Art, Rogers Fund, 1909.)

Figure 1-12. Tatted caps, each about 8 inches deep, Irish, nineteenth century. (Courtesy of the Metropolitan Museum of Art. Gift by subscription, 1909. Blackborne Collection.)

Figure 1-13. Nineteenth-century Irish tatting imitated lace. The second piece from the bottom, on the right, is a tatted cuff, 12 x 6 inches. (Courtesy of the Metropolitan Museum of Art. Gift of Mrs. Nuttall, 1908.)

There have been many attempts to trace the origins of tatting to macramé, or to a common ancestor. Macramé developed into its present form in southern Europe sometime during the fifteenth or sixteenth centuries, and the forerunners from which it evolved probably all belonged in the category of knotted textiles or their rudiments. It is true that macramé sometimes uses the same knot as tatting, the reversed double half hitch, as well as the term *tatted* to describe those knots. But the knots are essentially different from tatting because they use only an elementary direct method of tying, and the term *tatted* for the macramé knots does not seem to go back even as far as the last century. They were previously called *double buttonhole knots* by some experts.

Rather than macramé, it is decorative knotting that appears to be the ancestor of tatting. Knot tying is an extremely ancient craft. Knot records were used extensively all over the world as a primitive system of writing and for tallying. When Chinese decorative knotting appeared in the west in the 1690s, the knots were being tied in a complicated, sophisticated fashion that allowed them to be made very quickly and easily, a circumstance that probably reflects centuries of knot-tying technology, and without which the art could not have developed into tatting.

During the nineteenth century, the popularity of tatting alternately rose and fell. Some of the innovations may have been lost during the times that tatting was unpopular, for, as late as 1910 in England, and even today, we find quite a few individuals who can do no more than use a single shuttle to make the simplest tatted edgings, although more advanced techniques are known.

So far in its history, tatting had been only a pastime, and the product was not considered to have any great monetary value. In 1847, however, following the failure of the potato crop in Ireland, tatting was introduced at Ardee as one of the many cottage lace industries that were springing up in answer to the need for famine relief. The venture was only moderately successful and insignificant in relation to the rest of the Irish lace trade. However, Irish tatting was entered as lace in several international exhibitions, and, toward the end of the century, there were attempts to improve the monotonous circular designs. The Irish tatting industry, like the Irish crochet industry, was competing with manufacturers of other laces, and this must have played a role in the vogue for using extremely fine thread and in the deliberate attempts to imitate various kinds of lace.

Tatting in the Americas

Tatting is known and practiced everywhere in the United States. Members of one family in Maine have been tatting since before the Civil War — the men as well as the women. In a Pacific coast museum, one can find the fine, lovely work of Elizabeth Harpole Bayley, an Oregon pioneer. In fact, most American museums have examples of tatting, even if only as trimming for dolls' clothes. Tatting can also be found in both English and French Canada and in South America.

This range is not surprising. Tatting skills were undoubtedly brought along with the colonists from Europe, even though embroidery and lace were frowned on in early New England. Furthermore, American colonists of the upper classes frequently traveled to England. In 1784, Boswell records, he and Dr. Johnson met an American lady who was knotting while riding in a public coach in England.

As in Europe, periods when tatting was obscure alternated with periods of great popularity. In 1843, a set of needlework-instruction books published in New York included tatting, and two decades later, at the time of the Civil War, "Everybody wore tatting and almost everybody made it," wrote Clara Morris, an actress who lived then in Ohio. "I worked day and night at it, tatted at rehearsal and between scenes, and lady-stars often bought my work, to my great pleasure and profit."

Shortly before, in 1853, a book by Mrs. Pullan, a popular needlework authority, was published, including a section on tatting. The picot is discussed, and it is regarded primarily as a means of joining, but its use as an ornament is also mentioned. Instructions are given for only one design, a trimming that is strongly reminiscent of eyelet embroidery. The directions are quaint and unfamiliar, describing a technique that is no longer used today. Figure 3-48 is a picture of this edging, and modern directions for the project are given on page 56.

Figures 1-14, 1-15, 1-16. Handkerchief, handkerchief detail, and cruciform doily by Elizabeth Harpole Bayley. (Courtesy of Lincoln County Historical Museum, Newport, Oregon.)

Fig. 1-14

Fig. 1-15

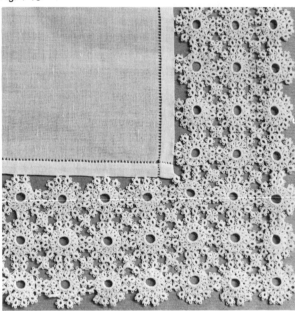

Fig. 1-16

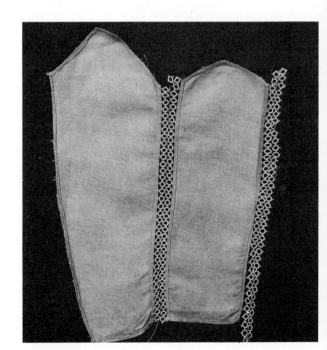

Figure 1-18. Napkin with surface embroidery, drawn-thread work, and tatted border, by Mrs. Frederica Keilson, Rio de Janeiro. Mrs. Keilson, who was born in Russia, saw tatting for the first time in Poland, but learned to do it in Brazil. (Courtesy of Joyce Pytkowicz.)

Figure 1-19. Tatting skills were carried back and forth between Great Britain and America in the eighteenth century. This wooden tatting bobbin from old New York traditionally belonged to Mrs. Philip Rhinelander (married 1784.) (Courtesy of Museum of the City of New York. Gift of Mrs. John Frelinghuysen Talmage, 1933.)

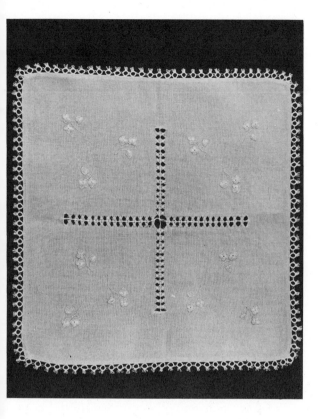

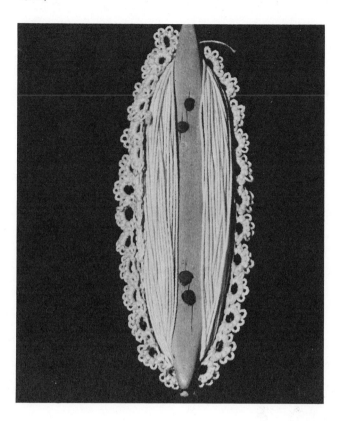

Figure 1-17. Tatting used as fagotting, a common practice of the time, on a fragment of bodice from French Canada, by Yvonne Saint-Pierre, 1910. (Courtesy of the National Museums of Canada.)

Figures 1-20, 1-21. Chemise with tatted cloverleaf trim, mid-nineteenth century. (Courtesy of The Costume and Textile Study Collection, School of Home Economics, University of Washington. Photograph by William Eng.)

Fig. 1-20

Fig. 1-21

Figure 1-22. Detail of baby's flannel skirt or petticoat with tatted cloverleaf trim, 1850—65. Stitched-on braid forms the leafy border, and feather-stitching is worked along the seams and hem. (Courtesy of The Costume and Textile Study Collection, School of Home Economics, University of Washington. Photograph by William Eng.)

Peterson's Magazine, one of the widely circulated ladies' magazines of the era, published another edging by Mrs. Pullan in March, 1857, which was to be worked in "rather coarse" cotton. Figure 1-23 shows an example worked from the instructions given, and left incomplete to show the unfamiliar construction. A row of rings is tatted, leaving a length of thread between them. Knots are then worked over the spaces to make chains, but, unlike modern tatted chains, without changing the bearing thread—the single thread that carries the knots. As each ring is reached, a further series of rings is worked around it.

The enormously popular *Godey's Ladies' Magazine* also published tatted designs. One in 1861 is a simple single-thread piece consisting of a series of rings, each with five picots, and separated by a length of thread. Interestingly, the picots are not used to join the rings, which are separate. Another, in 1864, is a single-thread design with no picots. The rings, again separated with a length of thread, are placed alternately up and down. Obviously this was meant to be sewn to a background.

In the twentieth century, tatting has been popular on and off. A minor revival occurred in the twenties, and, in the thirties and forties, thread manufacturers published pattern books with new designs, which did nothing to give tatting a new concept although they gave the work something of a new look. Since World War II, tatting has again been dormant.

Figure 1-23. Tatted edging worked from an 1857 pattern by Mrs. Pullan, a needlework expert.

Figure 1-24. Lappet by Elizabeth Bachelder of Andover, New Hampshire, around 1860—70. (Courtesy of Museum of Fine Arts, Boston.)

Figure 1-25. Late nineteenth-century tatting used as applied decoration and as border trim on a background which was originally a flour sack. (Courtesy of Oregon Historical Society.)

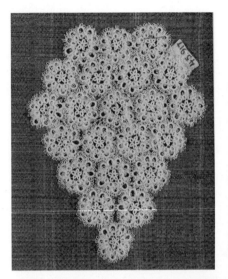

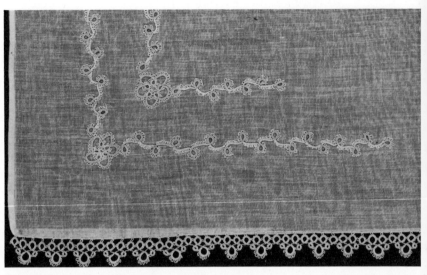

Figure 1-26. Detail of piano scarf, about 1925. Older designs, such as have been illustrated earlier in the chapter, were still popular in the twenties. (Courtesy of Bessie G. Murphy.)

Figure 1-27. Collar, late nineteenth or early twentieth century. Irish influence and a typical monotony of design are apparent. Pattern books of the period show much more variety, so perhaps people learned to tat from each other, following the fashion, rather than from books. (Courtesy of The Costume and Textile Study Collection, School of Home Economics, University of Washington. Photograph by William Eng.)

Figure 2-1. Side and front view of a pair of shuttles which are about 75 years old. Actual size is about 3¼ inches long. Although horn was frequently used at the time, the black material these are made from may be a synthetic. (Courtesy of Ruth Lines Motley.)

Figure 2-2. Two decorated shuttles, both about 2¾ inches and both about 50 years old. The German silver (nickel) shuttle on left is courtesy Ruth Lines Motley; the sterling silver shuttle on right is courtesy Sadie G. Allison.

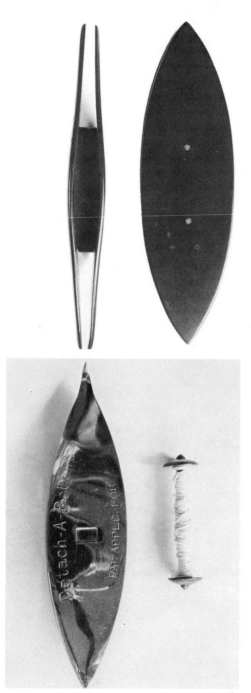

Figure 2-3. A metal shuttle with pick and detachable bobbin, which probably dates from the twenties. (Courtesy of Ruth Lines Motley.)

2/Tools and Materials

Contemporary forms of tatting were slow to develop because almost everyone believes that the traditional tool, the shuttle, is indispensable. This is not so! In fact, for learning to tat, it is far better to use only cotton parcel-post twine, preferably in two contrasting colors, and, if a crochet hook or knitting needle is not on hand, a round wooden toothpick. Working with heavy twine makes learning the basic knot easy, and the toothpick or crochet hook is used for joining sections of the work to each other. This cotton twine comes in white and, under the name of garden twine, in green. Cotton macramé cord, which appears to be no different, is available in many colors and can be purchased in craft and hobby shops. Buy two colors that can be easily distinguished. If something else must be substituted, choose a cotton cord smooth and strong enough to withstand heavy pulling without breaking. Some materials are difficult to tat with, and should be avoided by beginners. Their use is discussed later in the section on contemporary tatting.

Shuttles and Threads for Beginners

Once the rudiments have been learned, tools for contemporary or traditional work can be purchased inexpensively. The basic implement, the shuttle, is a convenient device for winding several yards of thread. Its boat shape allows it to move back and forth between the fingers with great speed. Complex patterns use two at once, and a pair of shuttles is often needed.

Regardless of what kind of tatting is planned in the long run, the reader should learn to use the shuttle and practice with it until it can be manipulated easily. This will not take a long time, and is especially important before attempting to work with the improvised tools recommended later for contemporary work. It will make it easier to use them and will also give some insight into their limitations so that, hopefully, better ones can be devised. It is not a good idea to use fine thread for this initial practice. However, most shuttles are made for fine thread only, and choice of both thread and shuttle must therefore be a compromise.

The heaviest thread that can be used conveniently in any of the shuttles currently available is 6-cord mercerized crochet cotton, size 3 (fig. 2-4). This thread is available from DMC, and comes in white and ecru. It is widely available locally in needlework and department stores, although not usually in variety stores, and may be ordered by mail. Several balls of this cotton, which are relatively small, will be needed for practice and for completing an initial project, such as one of the small bags in figs. 3-45, 3-46, or 3-47. Should this thread be unobtainable locally, order five or six balls by mail. A list of suppliers has been provided at the back of this book. At least three of the balls should be the same color to complete the project, allowing margin for error. For thread of this thickness, a fine needle and sewing thread that matches the tatting cotton in color are needed to finish the work off neatly.

Buy a pair of red plastic shuttles like those shown in Figure 2-4. These are two and three-quarter inches long, not counting the point, and can usually be purchased at almost any needlework counter throughout the country. Should there be any difficulty in finding them, check the list of suppliers at the end of this book. Smaller shuttles, or the metal type with a removable bobbin, will not accomodate a sufficient supply of size 3 thread and cannot be used for this purpose. However, those who own heirloom shuttles at least three inches long (fig. 2-5) already have ideal tools. Since many of these are

Figure 2-4. Once the fundamentals have been learned with the aid of string and toothpicks, these tools and materials are best for beginners: a few balls of 6-cord mercerized crochet cotton size 3 (DMC), two plastic shuttles, and two yarn bobbins like those used for knitting (optional). Ruler is included to show the size of the tools.

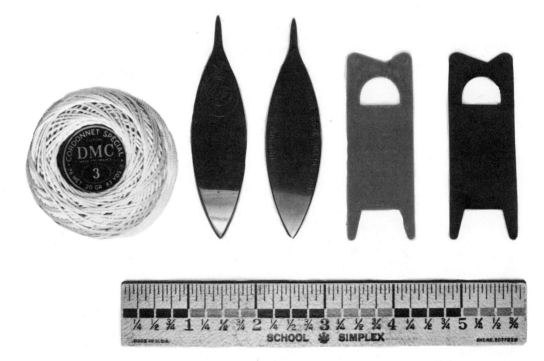

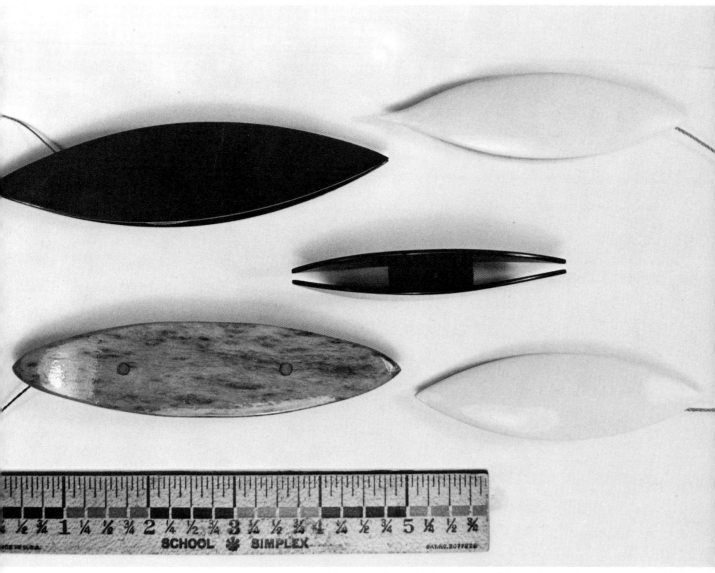

Figure 2-5. Older shuttles are generally larger than contemporary ones, and will hold a greater amount of thread. These are at least 3 inches long, and if smaller, as the one in the center, are open at the tips. (Large black shuttle given to author by Sadie G. Allison.)

Figure 2-6. Winding the shuttle. Pass the thread through the narrow slits at the ends, even though they appear to be tightly closed.

Tools and Materials for Traditional Tatting

Many young people today want to turn out needlework as much like that of their ancestors as possible. For fine tatting, of those shuttles now on the market, the ones pictured in Fig. 2-8 will be found best. Do not pile tatting cotton up beyond the edges of the tool, since the sides protect white or light-colored materials from soil and unnecessary friction. The removable bobbin of the metal shuttle should never be filled much more than three-quarters full, or the thread may slip between bobbin and shuttle causing a black mark that is practically impossible to remove. To wind the metal shuttle, remove the bobbin in the center by pushing hard against it with the thumb. Wind the thread around the bobbin and then snap it back into the shuttle. If there are holes in the shuttle, there is no need to put the thread through them.

The thread most commonly used for tatted lace is 6-cord mercerized crochet cotton, finer than the DMC size 3. It comes in various thicknesses from an even heavier size 1 to a very fine 150. This must not be confused with 3-cord mercerized crochet cotton which looks the same and comes in many of the same sizes but which is not as suitable for tatting, since rings made with it can be difficult to close. The 6-cord crochet cotton comes only in white or ecru, except for size 70, and, in DMC sizes 30 and 50. Fine white or colored tatting cotton, such as Coats and Clark's tatting-crochet size 70, can be bought almost anywhere, as can sizes 20 and 30 in white or ecru.

Pearl cotton, because it is readily available and comes in a variety of lustrous colors, though few sizes, (3, 5, and 8 now being the most common) is sometimes used for traditional tatting. Fabrics knotted with it do not have the crisp look that is achieved with 6-cord, and they quickly become fuzzy with use. It is therefore not recommended as a substitute, although it may be used in other ways, such as for padding or in contemporary work.

without points, a small crochet hook, of a size for fine threads, will be needed for joining. Some older shuttles, though not quite this long, are open at the tips and will also serve (fig. 2-5, center). Be careful, however, not to ruin a small old shuttle that closes firmly at the tips by winding it with the thick material recommended here.

To wind any of these shuttles, hold the very end of the tatting cotton against the edge of the tool with the left thumb, and keep it there until enough turns have been made around the center post to secure the thread so that it no longer slips (fig. 2-6). The thread will pass easily through the narrow slits at either end of the shuttle, even though they appear to be tightly closed. Do not bother with the hole in the post if there is one, and do not tie the end around the post. This is unnecessary, and it is a nuisance to have to stop and cut a knot each time the thread on the shuttle runs out. Continue to wind as evenly as possible, until the shuttle is filled. For the time being, do not pile tatting cotton up beyond the edges of the shuttle, although this rule will sometimes have to be broken later.

Though not the preferred choice for this practice, two yarn bobbins like those shown in Figure 2-4 can be substituted for the shuttles. They are sold as knitting tools. To use a yarn bobbin for this purpose, wind the thread around it, and, holding it flat with the little "feet" toward the palm of the hand, use it exactly like a shuttle. Here again, a crochet hook will be needed.

Figure 2-8. Small shuttles (these are about 2½ inches) are suitable for fine tatting, because a sufficient length of fine thread can be wound onto them. The metal shuttle at right has a removable bobbin.

Figure 2-7. Traditional threads were much finer than those used today. In this incredibly fine piece of tatting from Winnipeg the thread is finer than any available now. (Given to the author for her collection by the late E. Lolita Eveleth.)

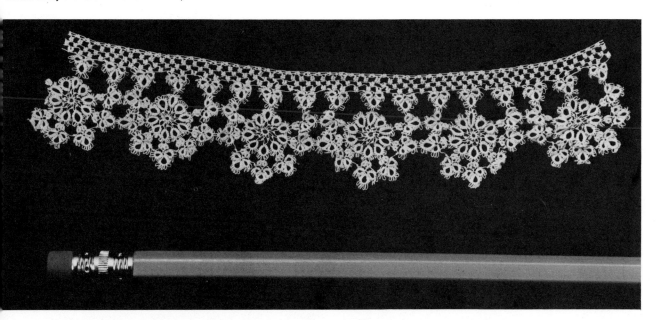

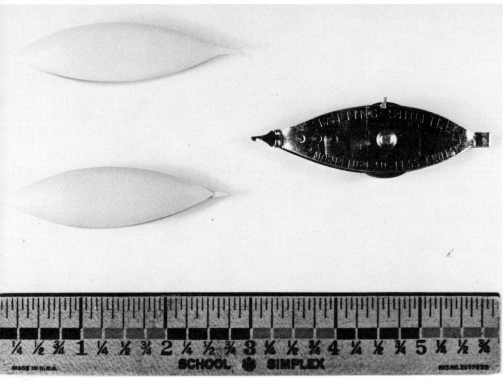

Tools and Materials for Contemporary Tatting

Even when doing more traditional work, there is no reason to keep to the old standbys. All sorts of threads have been used for tatting in the past, and, today, interesting trimmings result when rami or fine crewel embroidery wool are used for edgings. Three-ply polypropylene knitting yarn can be split and wound on shuttles to achieve a translucent effect quite unlike ordinary tatting (fig. 2-9). Try whatever smooth linen comes to hand, and those who have access to a supply of linen lace thread should certainly use it for tatting. Rayon and nylon, while they can often be used in the conventional shuttle, present special problems which will be discussed later.

When working with yarns much thicker than the traditional tatting cotton, none of the shuttles currently available will do, and all the tools must be improvised. To begin with, lay in a supply of rubber bands in various sizes, and a pair of yarn bobbins, jumbo size (fig. 2-11). These are much larger than the yarn bobbins described earlier (see fig. 2-4), and are sold as tools for bulky knitting. One manufacturer makes a shorter, wider style, which some readers may want to try, although those with small hands may find them difficult to manipulate. Instructions for the use of these tools are supplied in Chapter 4, where methods for making other improvised tools are given along with a discussion of what materials to use.

As you learn the techniques of tatting, you will see that large areas are most often created by joining together similar, smaller tatted motifs or strips of tatting. When using fine material, motifs can usually be created with only one shuttle full of thread, and the whole piece often takes only a few balls of thread. Therefore, estimating the amount of material to be used in a project is generally not as crucial as in crocheting or knitting, where many skeins of the same dyelot must be purchased at one time. When using more contemporary, bulkier materials for tatting, however, some of these same problems may be encountered. Instructions for estimating length by making a sample swatch are given on page 68. A deep box, at least as large as a shoebox, perhaps with a slot cut in the top, will be found useful for keeping tatted swatches together in one place.

Figure 2-9. Materials for contemporary tatting can be thick and made of synthetics. This sachet was made of 3-ply polypropylene knitting yarn, split and wound on a shuttle. (Courtesy of Susan E. Munstedt.)

Figure 2-10. White nylon stitching twine gives an entirely different look than traditional thread in the same pattern. Full piece is shown in Figure 7-4.

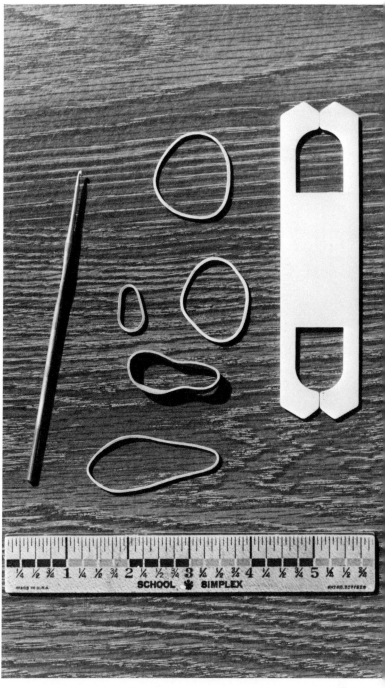

Figure 2-11. Tools for contemporary tatting: a small crochet hook for joining, rubber bands for securing balls of yarn as in a shuttle substitute, and jumbo yarn bobbins, which are sold as tools for bulky knitting, and serve as shuttle substitutes for fuzzy yarns.

Accessories and Other Materials

If a crochet hook is used for tatting, it is a good idea to hang it around the neck or to suspend a shortened version from a bracelet worn on the right wrist. In the latter case, the bracelet must be long enough so that the tool can be flipped into the hand when needed. A less well-known device is the pin and ring used in the nineteenth century. It is more convenient than it sounds, and it can be made by tying a blunt-pointed tapestry needle to a nine-inch length of crochet cotton (fig 2-12). Make a loop at the other end and slip it over the left thumb. There should be about five inches of cord between the needle and the ring.

Most people quickly learn to make picots that are uniform in size. If necessary, a paper clip or something similar can be used as a gauge or spacer by inserting it between the ring and shuttle threads and drawing the knot that follows the picot up close to it. This gives confidence at first, but it slows up the work and puts off the day when one can make evenly sized picots without a crutch. However, for making picots in graduated sizes, and such designs can be spectacular, gauges are invaluable.

Beads and sequins or any found objects that either have or can have holes drilled in them may be used to enhance tatting. In almost every case, the holes must be large enough to accomodate the thread used for the tatting after it has been doubled. For tatted jewelry, handcrafted findings, which are generally much more satisfactory than commercial ones, can be devised.

Commercial braids and other trimmings can also be combined with tatting. This is an old practice, and nowadays, we might consider using various kinds of lace as well.

It is hard to list the many items that might profitably be kept on hand by the tatter whose approach is truly experimental. Materials such as the soft cord used in dressmaking can be used for padding tatted rings and chains. Threads might be dyed, perhaps using different colors to produce variegated threads or other effects. Tatting can be suspended from dowels or hoops, and in three-dimensional work, wire, wood, or other materials for making armatures should be on hand. Substances like dipping plastic can entirely change the character of the work, and are fun to try.

Several methods of finishing work are described in Chapter 8, and the usual pins, sewing, and gluing materials will be needed, as well as whatever backing material might be wanted. Before mounting, it may be advisable to treat the fabric with one of the various sprays that protect or enhance the finish.

Those who wish to decorate writing paper, bulletin boards, scrapbook covers, or other objects with tatted motifs may want ink, paints, and scraps of colorful fabric, lace, or ribbon.

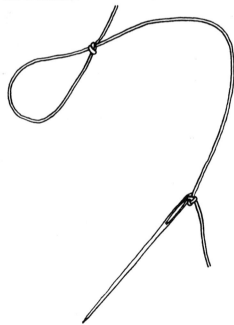

Figure 2-12. The ring and pin, a simple but effective traditional tool for joining.

Figure 2-13. Hand-decorated letter paper serves as backing for tatted flowers. (Courtesy of Rachel Wareham.)

Figure 3-1. Circular doily, early twentieth century, by Elizabeth
Harpole Bayley. Notice how the intricate pattern is formed entirely
of rings joined by picots. (Courtesy of Lincoln County Historical
Museum, Newport, Oregon.)

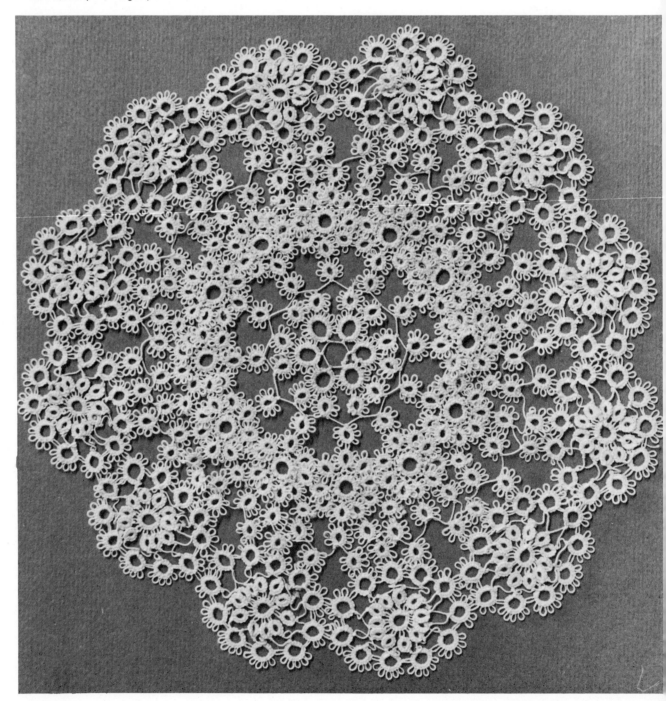

3/The Familiar Snowflake

Basic techniques

The basic knot. For all its elaborate appearance, tatting is nothing more than the repetition of a single knot, one with which almost everybody is familiar. The knot can be tied in more than one way. In tatting, it is made in an indirect, somewhat complicated fashion. This widens its scope and allows it to be used to form, along a single thread, a series of circles or rings which can be closely spaced and quickly worked.

Cut two lengths of cotton parcel-post twine or other heavy cord, each about eight inches long and each of a different color. Lay one aside. Fold the other in half and wrap it, doubled, once around a pencil or other rigid object, slipping both ends of the twine through the loop and pulling tight (fig. 3-2). The result is a cow hitch, the knot used for baggage tags.

The cow hitch can also be made in two motions by taking a reversed double half hitch around the pencil, as in Figure 3-3. This consists of two half hitches, the first represented in the diagram by solid lines, the second by broken lines. Notice that the cord goes first *over* the pencil and back under it (to the left), then *under* and back over (to the right). Thus the two halves of the knot are mirror images of each other. Compare

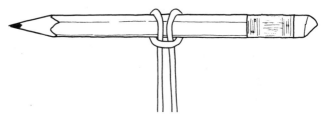

Figure 3-2. The cow hitch, basic knot used in tatting. The pencil is used, for beginning practice, in place of another cord.

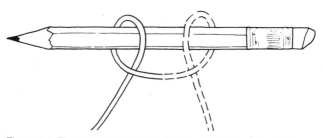

Figure 3-3. The reversed double half hitch, essentially a cow hitch tied in two separate motions. Parts of knot are mirror images.

this with the two sets of double half hitches in Figure 3-4, neither of which forms a cow hitch, because in both knots the two halves of the pair are identical.

The tatting knot is a cow hitch that has been made over a running line. Slip the twine off the pencil, and tie a knot as before, but this time substitute the second eight-inch piece of twine for the pencil (fig. 3-5). This second piece of twine over which the knot is now tied has been converted to a running line, also called a *knot-bearer* or *knot-carrier*. Notice that the knot slides back and forth easily along it.

It will simplify matters always to think of the tatting knot as a reversed double half hitch. The most common name for it is *double stitch*, and, indeed, it can only be made in two motions as in Figure 3-3. Incidentally, though knot terminology varies considerably, when the knot and the knot-bearer are both part of one continuous cord, as they are when making tatted rings, the name of the knot changes to *ring knot* or *lark's head*.

Returning to the model represented in Figure 3-5, take the two ends of the twine that *form* the knot, and, grasping one in each hand, pull them straight out in opposite directions as indicated by the arrows. Let the ends of the running line fall where they may. Pull tightly. The piece held will straighten itself, and the other piece will form a new knot once the ends are pulled straight. This new knot is identical, once the ends are straightened, to the one that was pulled out; the formation is still a cow hitch on a running line, except that the cord that was previously the knot-bearer has become the one that forms the knot, and vice versa (fig. 3-6).

This reversal, which is referred to as *changing the knot-bearer,* or *reversing the bearing thread*, can be carried on indefinitely from one cord to the other, or on two alternate sections of a continuous cord. The result will always be the same: *The slack cord forms the knot; the cord that has been pulled taut is the knot-bearer.*

This principle applies to the tatting knot and to its component part, the half hitch, as well. It is very important to the tatter — more important, in fact, than the shuttle, which, as you have seen, is not essential to making the basic knot in tatting.

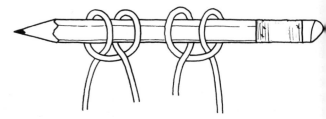

Figure 3-4. Double half hitches. Parts of knot are identical, and do not form a cow hitch.

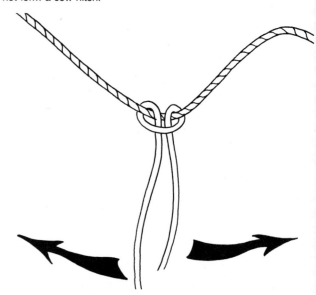

Figure 3-5. A cow hitch tied over a running line. Pull the ends of the knot straight out to the sides as indicated by the arrows, to reverse the knot and knot-bearer.

Figure 3-6. The bearing thread is now reversed. The slack thread forms the knot; the thread that has been pulled taut is the knot-bearer. This principle applies to the cow hitch and all half hitches, and this reversed knot is the basic tatting stitch.

The ring.   Now that you know how to make a cow hitch with two separate cords, let us see how the knot is made and the bearing thread reversed when using a single continuous thread for both knot and knot-bearer. Cut off about three-quarters of a yard of one color of cotton parcel-post twine. Grasp it three inches or so from one end, between the thumb and forefinger of the left hand. The short end should point toward the floor. Carry the rest of the twine over the backs of the half-bent fingers of the left hand toward the little finger. Hold forefinger and middle finger apart so there is a good space between them. Continue threading around the little finger, back under the other fingers toward the thumb, then catching the twine again between thumb and forefinger, so that there is a ring around the hand (fig. 3-7). This will be referred to from now on as the *ring thread*. Do not confuse it with the term *ring* which refers to the tatted rings that will be made. The portion of the twine that runs from the left thumb and forefinger to the right hand is called the *shuttle thread*. Once work has begun, the ring thread must be held closed by the thumb and forefinger, without letting go, until the two parts of the first knot are completed.

With the right hand, pick up the end of the long, free section of the cord, the shuttle thread, put it *under* and then bring it back *over* the part of the ring thread that stretches between the index and the middle fingers, and, finally, take it, in the direction shown, through the loop that has resulted, but do not tighten the knot that is forming (fig. 3–8). Observe that the ring thread is taut and that the shuttle thread twists around it in a half hitch. This will not work. Instead, the shuttle thread must become the knot-bearer and the ring thread must be made to twist around it. We already know how to do that: The slack thread forms the knot; the thread that has been pulled taut is the knot-bearer.

Therefore, without letting the ring thread slip off, the fingers of the left hand must be relaxed, and the thread in the right

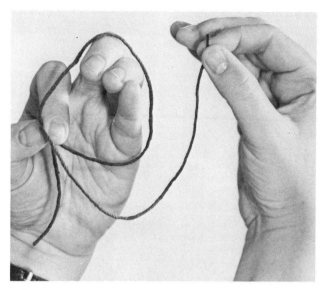

Figure 3-7. Making a ring, starting position. The cord around the fingers is the *ring thread*; the cord running from left thumb and forefinger to right hand is the *shuttle thread*.

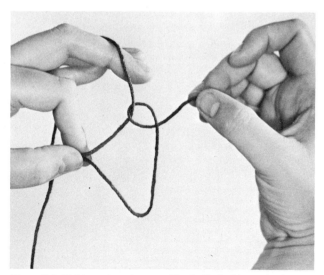

Figure 3-8. Making a ring, step one. The first half of the tatting knot in progress, with the knot-bearer not yet reversed. To reach this position take the shuttle thread first under the ring thread, then back over it and through the loop.

hand pulled tight (fig. 3-9). Be careful! At this point, the knot has a very strong tendency to revert, and only a slight tightening of the fingers of the left hand combined with very little relaxation of the shuttle thread will cause it to do so. Allow this to happen to see the result, then reverse the knot-bearer again so the knot is correct. Do it several times; it develops control.

Finally, with the knot in the correct position, tighten it, at the same time sliding it to the left so that it can be held in place by the thumb and forefinger of the left hand (fig. 3-10). This will be difficult at first. For the time being, get it there any way that seems easy without letting the knot-bearer reverse again. Later, after a little practice, you will find that the knot glides along the knot-bearer if the middle finger of the left hand is raised slowly, while keeping a very tight hold on the cord in the right hand so that it does not become slack. Should the knot stick, it can be helped along by moving the still tightly held shuttle thread up and down in an arc. Never move it toward or away from the worker, since, in the hand of a beginner, this is tantamount to letting it go slack. When the knot is in position, test it as shown, to be sure the cord in the right hand will pull (fig. 3-11).

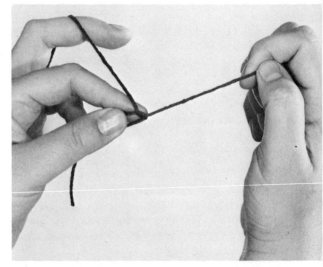

Figure 3-10. Making a ring, step three. Move the reversed knot to the left where it can be held in place by the left thumb and forefinger. A correctly formed knot slides along the knot bearer easily, and the cord in the right hand slips easily through the knot when pulled to the right.

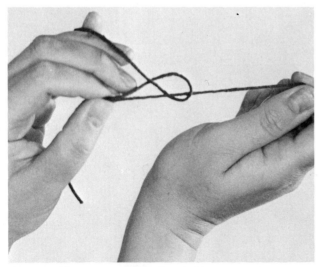

Figure 3-9. Making a ring, step two. Reversing the first half of the knot. Relax the fingers of the left hand, pull the cord in the right hand taut. Changing the knot-bearer is the most important step in making a tatted ring; when people fail to learn tatting, it is because they have overlooked this point.

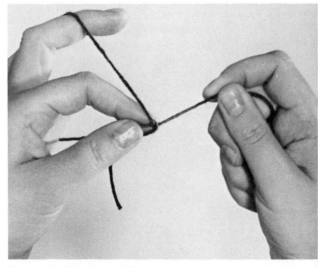

Figure 3-11. Steps two and three, when done incorrectly, prevent the knot from sliding along the knot bearer, and the cord will not pull to the right. Either the knot-bearer was not changed, or the knot was allowed to snap back into the wrong position.

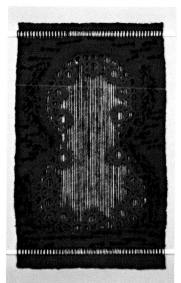

Hourglass, woven tapestry featuring two kinds of tatting. The tatted shape of cotton cable twist was made first. Then, as the weaving progressed, its edges were caught in place as the weft was worked. Knotted lines were used as part of the weft. (Courtesy of Vivian Poon.)

Autumn Rain, a woven tapestry with tatted rings, hung by means of tatted rings. (Courtesy of Vivian Poon.)

Wall hanging of couched knotting and tatted rings of viscose straw, applied to burlap. A row of glued-on pebbles supplies weight and hides knots. (Courtesy of Lynda Ford Voris.)

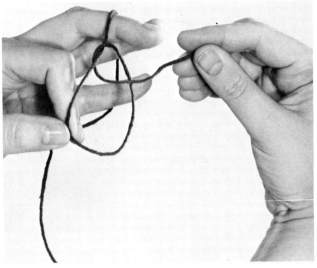

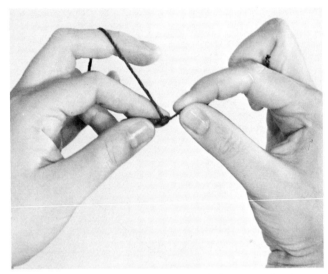

Figure 3-12. Step four. The second half of the tatting knot in progress with the knot-bearer not yet reversed. This time the shuttle thread goes *over* the ring thread first, then comes back *under* it and through the loop. Afterwards, this knot is also pushed to the left.

Figure 3-13. The first tatting knot completed. Test to see that the shuttle thread pulls easily. If not, begin again with a new length of cord, and pay special attention to the instructions for changing the knot-bearer.

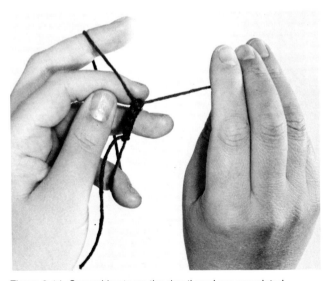

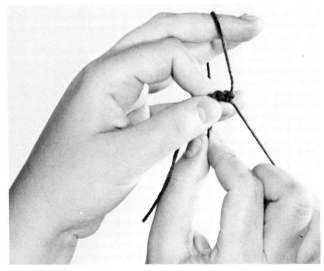

Figure 3-14. Several knots on the ring thread are completed.

Figure 3-15. When the ring thread becomes too tight, hold the knots firmly as shown and pull on cord to left of knots to ease more thread into the circle around the fingers. Then begin tatting again.

To make the second half of the knot, the shuttle thread goes first *over* and then comes back *under* the ring thread, again going through the loop that is formed (fig. 3-12). Once more the knot-bearer must be changed, as it must for every knot made, and once more the tatter must resist its tendency to revert until the second half of the knot is tightened and safely positioned next to the first half (fig. 3-13). After this, the ring thread need not be held so carefully with the fingers; it is now held closed by the knot. The shuttle thread should still pull easily to the right. Test it to be sure it does.

Continue making double knots, placing them close to each other as shown in Figure 3-14. If the thread around the fingers becomes too tight, slide it open by pulling on it to the left of the knots (fig. 3-15). Finally, after about ten knots are completed, close the ring. This is done by holding the knots firmly and pulling on the right-hand cord. Usually, a better-shaped ring results if the first and last knots are brought together before this is done (fig. 3-16). Be sure the ring is closed all the way. None of the ring thread should be left showing at the base. Identical rings can be of vastly different sizes if they are not drawn up uniformly, so learn to pull rings up snugly. If the ring thread has any tendency to twist, stop and straighten it out before pulling it through any further. Otherwise, the cord may kink and prevent proper closing.

The beginner who understands this much is completely over the hump. There is nothing more to learn in tatting that is the least bit difficult or confusing. It is necessary, however, to practice making rings until it can be done quickly and easily. The position and movements of the left hand are, after all, completely new to most people. The best way to practice is to carry a few one-yard lengths of cord in a pocket so that you can practice in odd moments. Do not close the rings. Instead, open them all the way, and let the knots slide off. This is a good test of whether or not they were properly made, and the string can be used over again. If a mistake was made, and the ring will not pull, substitute a new cord.

The typical beginner has trouble remembering whether the last half hitch was taken over or under the cord, but, after relatively little practice, you will be able to tell merely by look-ing at the knots. When you have achieved some facility, it should be interesting for you to look back and compare the knots you are making with the one shown in Figure 3-3. Although the results are the same as making the simple cow hitch, not only is the knot-bearer changed, but the tatting knot is tied in an upside-down and backward sequence.

Figure 3-16. Making a ring, final step. After enough knots have been made, close the ring by pulling on the right-hand cord.

Tatted butterfly. Butterflies have long been favorite motifs in tatting. This one was worked from a cartoon and is made of nylon stitching twine, heavy silk, pearl cotton, stranded embroidery cotton, and copper wire. A bobble forms the body (see fig. 6-1).

Open shadow box, linen thread. Tatting combined with needlepoint lace forms a double layer which is fastened into a wooden frame. (Courtesy of Mieke Kerkstra.)

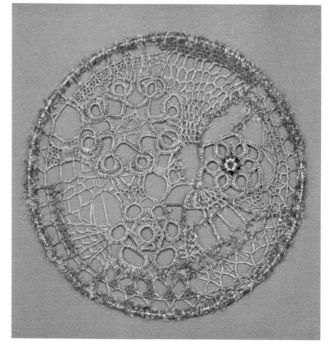

Circle, linen thread, fuzzy yarn, and a bead in a combination of tatting and needlepoint lace. (Courtesy of Mieke Kerkstra.)

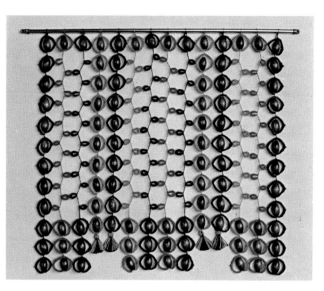

Wall hanging of rami and large wooden beads. The rami was used in a double strand. See pattern on page 101.

Shoulder-strap purse with tatted panel of cotton cable twist and ceramic beads. The purse itself was constructed from buckram covered with homespun and vinyl fabric. See pattern for tatted panel on page 97.

Figure 3-17. The picot. Rings and chains of tatting are joined to one another through these little loops left between knots.

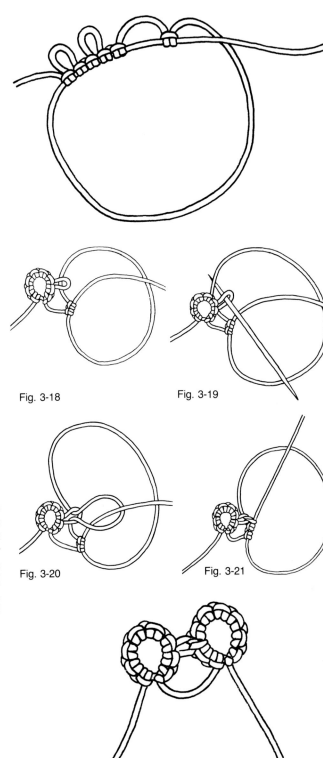

The picot. The word *picot* (pronounced PEA-COE) is a lace-making term that refers to any one of the tiny ornamental loops often found along the edges of lace or braid. The word was borrowed from the French only about 100 years ago, and it has completely replaced the earlier word *purl*. In tatting, too, the picot serves as an ornament. However, it has a more important function, that of a connecting device.

To form picots on the practice ring, make the knots as usual, but instead of running them up close to each other, leave spaces between them of a least half an inch. Then, when they are pushed together, the spaces will become picots (fig. 3-17). This may be done between every knot, or less often, as desired. Notice that picots are placed between whole knots and not between the two parts of the knot.

Two rings may be joined together if the first ring has a picot. To do this, use a one-yard cord and make a ring that consists of six knots, a picot, and two more knots. Close the ring and begin a second one, leaving a space between them of about half an inch. Put two knots on the new ring and attach it to the first as follows: without removing the work from the left hand, position the picot so that it lies over the ring thread close to where the last knot was tied (fig. 3-18). With a toothpick, draw the ring thread up through the picot far enough so that the shuttle thread can be passed through the loop that results (fig. 3-19 and 3-20). Finally, pull the cord in the right hand out straight and, at the same time, tighten the loop you pulled through the picot by stretching out the fingers of the left hand (fig. 3-21). Notice that, after the loop is back in position, the knot-bearer can still be pulled back and forth as before; the connection has not interfered with the ability to close the ring. It is possible to pull the loop back too far, thus forcing the bearing thread out of line. A slight opening or closing of the ring counteracts this, and beginners should do it before going on to the next knot. Make six more knots and close, as shown in Figure 3-22. If you want to add a third ring, instead of the six knots make four more, then a picot, and then two more knots before closing.

Fig. 3-18   Fig. 3-19

Fig. 3-20   Fig. 3-21

Figures 3-18, 3-19, 3-20, and 3-21. Joining a ring in progress to a completed ring by means of a picot. A toothpick, a pin, a crochet hook, or a hook on a tatting shuttle may be used to pull up the ring thread through the picot.

Figure 3-22. Joining completed. After both the ring thread and the shuttle thread have been drawn back into place, continue tatting as before, to complete the ring.

The chain. In tatting, knots are not always worked in rings. As the art developed, people also began using two threads to make straight lines or *chains*. In the first set of instructions that follow, be sure to use two colors as directed, in order to see clearly which cord is forming the knots. The different cords will help you gain some understanding of how color distributes itself in tatting, in preparation for the time when you may want to use two-color designs like those in Figure 3-32.

There are two ways to begin a chain. For the first method, cut two lengths of cord, one light and one dark, each a half yard long. Grasp the dark cord between the left thumb and forefinger, and carry it over the backs of the fingers as though about to make a ring. Instead of taking it *over* the back of the little finger, however, carry it *under* (fig 3-23), and twist the cord twice around the top joint of the finger. Then bend the finger down to hold the cord securely (fig. 3-24). Some people find this position difficult at first, but it becomes easy with practice.

Now catch the light cord between the left thumb and forefinger also, and, taking the other end of this shuttle thread in the right hand (fig. 3-25), make tatting knots exactly as though working over a ring thread. Since the knot-bearer is changed as in making a ring, the knots are formed with the dark cord, and the tatting is the dark color, because the knot-bearer is almost entirely hidden. Picots may be made as desired (fig. 3-26).

For the second method, begin again, this time with a one-yard length of the light cord only. Start in the middle of the string and wrap half of it around the left hand as was done in making the first chain. Pick up the long end of the cord that dangles between thumb and forefinger, and, with it, make the first half of the knot (fig. 3-27). When pulled tight, it will look like the knot in Figure 3-28. Figure 3-29 shows the second half of the knot made and brought up close to the first. After that, there is something to hold on to, which makes things easier. When this method is used, the ends of thread at the beginning of the chain are eliminated, something which, in contemporary work, is often very desirable.

Chains may be joined to rings or to other chains by means of picots in the same way that rings are joined. In addition, the *shuttle* thread may be joined to a ring or chain (fig. 3-30).

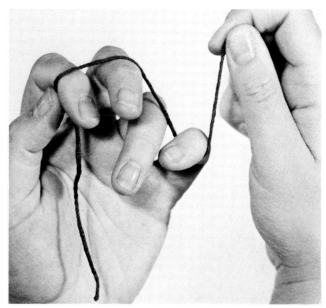

Figure 3-23. Making a chain, starting position. Two separate cords are used, and here the first is being wound around the fingers.

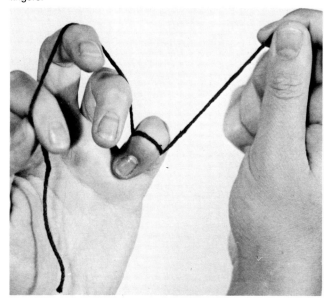

Figure 3-24. Making a chain, starting position. Continue winding the first cord around the little finger, then bend little finger down to hold it.

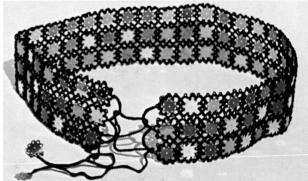

Belt of sequins held together with tatting. (Courtesy of Dorothy Tooker.)

Pendant and necklace of nylon stitching twine, small ceramic beads and imitation pearls. See pattern on page 103.

Pendant and necklace of nylon stitching twine and plastic cluster beads.

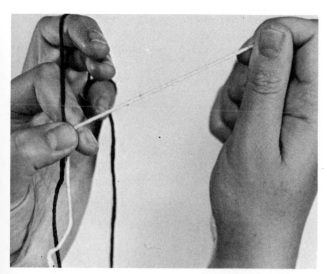

Figure 3-25. Making a chain, starting position. Grasp the second cord as shown. Two colors are used to help differentiate the parts of the knotted chain.

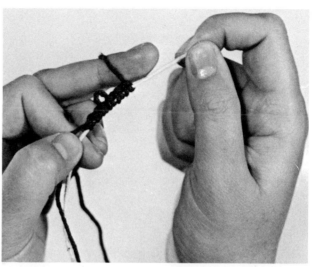

Figure 3-26. The chain in progress. The knots are formed exactly as on the ring, but the knot-bearer (light cord) is free at both ends. The knots are the color of the cord that was wound around the fingers. Picots are also made as in the ring.

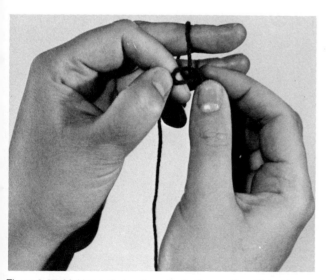

Figure 3-27. Making a chain, alternate starting position. To begin a chain in the middle of a continuous cord, thus eliminating ends, grasp the center between thumb and forefinger, wind one end around the little finger as before, and use the other end, instead of a separate cord, as the shuttle thread.

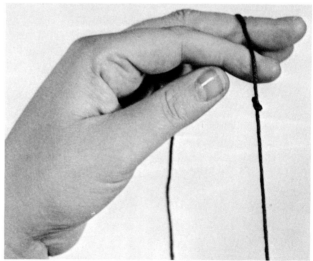

Figure 3-28. Making a chain with a continuous cord, step one. The first half of the knot is completed. As shown, it appears in the middle of the cord, but ordinarily it would remain between the thumb and the forefinger.

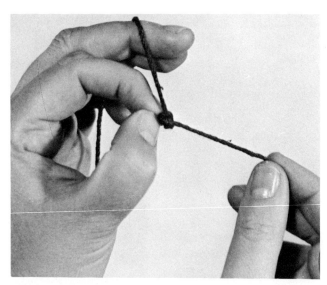

Figure 3-29. Making a chain with a continuous cord, step two. The second half of the knot is completed, to form the first double knot.

Figure 3-30. Joining the *shuttle* thread of a chain to a ring. Chains may be attached to rings or to other chains by means of picots, and either shuttle or ring thread may be used for the joining.

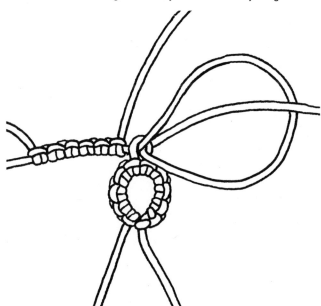

Chains and rings. There are tatted designs that consist entirely of rings, and some that consist entirely of chains. In most patterns, however, both are found, and one must know how to switch from one to the other. Here is the way it is most commonly done, although this is by no means the only way.

With a one-and-one-half-yard length of light-color cord, make a ring that consists of two knots, a picot, four knots, another picot, and two more knots. A string this long begins to be a little clumsy, but it can be managed. Close the ring, and turn it upside down (fig. 3-31). Without cutting any cord off the dark ball, take the end and lay it alongside the one on which the ring was made in the position shown. Holding both ring and dark cord together with the left thumb and forefinger, drape the dark cord over the back of the left hand in the position used for making chains. With the long end of the white cord, which is the shuttle thread, tat a chain of four knots, a picot, and four more knots. Again reverse the work, that is, turn it right side up in the position it was in when the ring was made. Still working with the light cord, make a second ring as follows: tat two knots, join to the second picot of the first ring without twisting the chain, make four more knots, a picot, two knots, and close the ring. Again reverse the work, and repeat the chain. Reverse again, and continue in this way until the light string becomes too short, when there will probably be four rings and three chains (fig. 3-32a). Observe that the formation has a distinct tendency to curve. A complete circle could be made, had the cord not run out. The last ring could then also be attached to the first picot of the first ring.

Make a second series of rings and chains, this time using either ball of cord, but do not cut off a length to work with. Instead, merely unroll about two yards and make the first ring about a yard and a half from the end. Make the chains in this new series only four knots long. When the first ring is completed, reverse, and begin the first chain. Work over the part of the cord that leads to the ball, and push the first knot of the chain up close to the base of the ring. Continue, always reversing the work, until five rings and four chains have been completed (fig. 3-32b). There are now no loose ends at the beginning of the strip, and the shorter chains have greatly counteracted the tendency of the formation to curve.

Figure 3-32. Ring and chain formations. Combinations include a pattern using two separate cords (a), a pattern made from a single continuous cord (b), and a pattern using two active cords, that is, one in which two shuttles or shuttle substitutes are needed (c).

Figure 3-31. A common procedure in tatting is to make a chain with a ball thread, after having made a ring. The ring is generally first turned upside-down, which is indicated by the instructions *reverse work*.

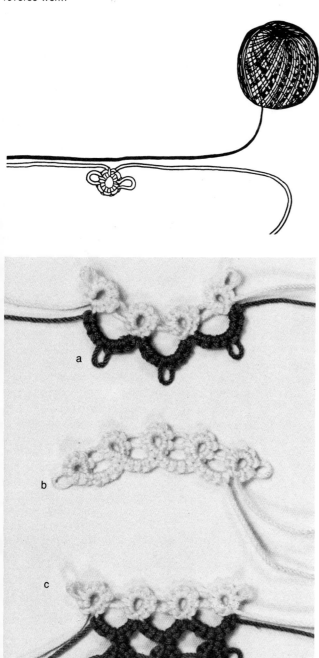

Working with two active cords. Begin again with two cords of different colors, each a yard and a half long. With the light color, make a ring of two knots, a picot, four knots, a second picot, and two more knots. Close the ring. Reverse the work, and, tatting over the dark cord, make a chain of three knots. Drop the light cord, and using the dark, *but without reversing the work*, form a new ring, exactly like the first. There should be no space between the second ring and the chain. Switch cords, and again without reversing, make three more knots with the light string over the dark. Reverse, and with the light make a second ring, attaching it, after the second knot, to the second picot of the first ring. Continue in this way, attaching the second dark ring to the first dark ring and the third light ring to the second light one. The series could go on indefinitely, but by now the length of dark string will have run out. The sample has light rings on one side, dark rings on the other, and the chains are dark (fig. 3-32c).

If you work this in one color with a two-yard length of cord, as shown in Figures 3-27 through 3-30, the ends that dangle from the starting side of the piece can be eliminated.

Using the shuttle. The basic processes of tatting have all been introduced, with the exception of how to secure ends. Little more can be accomplished with short lengths of cord; something on which several yards can be wound is necessary. This is the function of the tatting shuttle. It adds no new element; using it requires only a variation of basic skills you have already learned.

Use a shuttle like those shown in Figure 2-4, or substitute an older shuttle like those in Figure 2-5. Wind it, as described on page 26, with DMC 6-cord crochet cotton size 3. Hold it between the thumb and forefinger of the right hand, touching only the flat sides of the shuttle, not the edges (fig. 3-33). The point, or the hook if there is one, must always be forward, away from the hand, or the tatter risks a bad stab. Beginners usually find it easiest if the thread is allowed to escape from the shuttle, as shown in Figure 3-33: thread leaves the shuttle between the center post and the point on the open side of the shuttle that is away from the worker. Later this becomes less important. Keep the shuttle thread as short as is practical, because speed and facility are lost unless this is done.

Figures 3-34, 3-35, and 3-36 show the "easiest" way to handle the shuttle, but are incorrect. If you follow these movements, no knot will form. Although the shuttle goes under and comes back over the ring thread, it does not go through the loop. For it to do so from the final position resulting from these incorrect movements would require an extra

Figure 3-33. Using the shuttle, proper hand position.

Figures 3-34, 3-35, and 3-36. Although incorrect, this sequence of positions seems natural to beginners, and should be tried before going on to the correct way to form the knot with a shuttle.

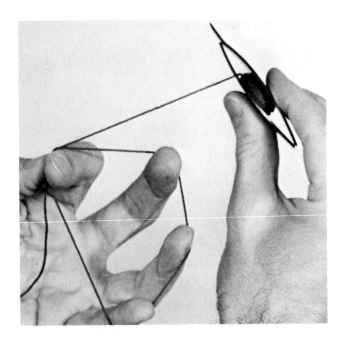

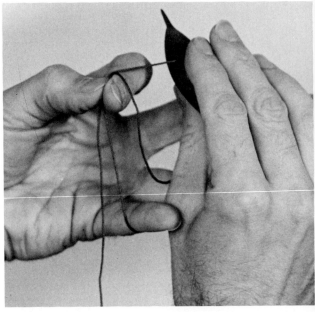

Fig. 3-34

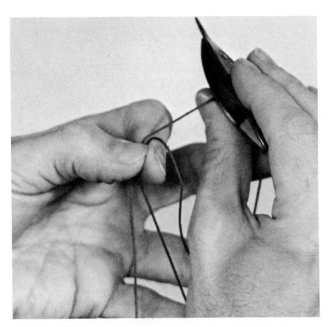

Fig. 3-35

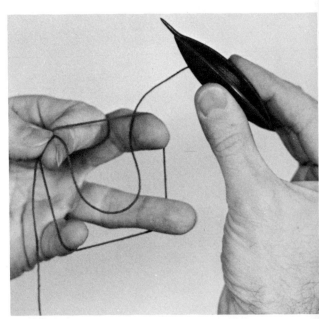

Fig. 3-36

Figure 3-37. Forming the knot with a shuttle, starting position. The right hand is turned palm upward, and the middle, ring finger, and little finger are folded over the shuttle thread.

Figure 3-39. Forming the knot with a shuttle, step three. To complete the second part of the first half of the knot, the shuttle comes back over the ring thread and through the loop automatically, without being twisted or turned in any way.

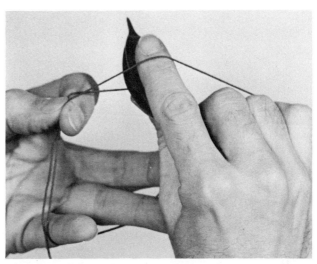

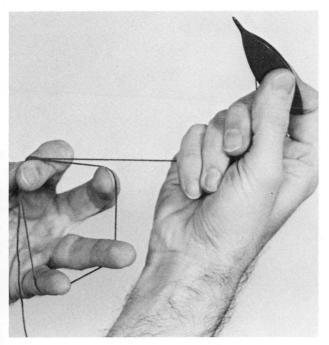

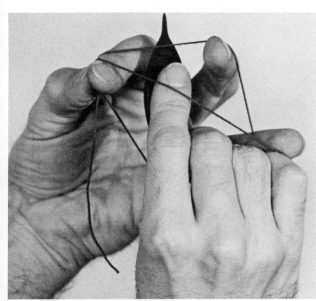

Figure 3-38. Forming the knot with a shuttle, step two. The shuttle thread is out of the way, over the backs of the fingers, as it goes under the ring thread.

motion and a clumsy one. Try this anyway, before going on to the proper position, to get the feel of the shuttle going under and over the ring thread. Taking the position shown in Figure 3-34, pass the shuttle under the ring thread and let the ring thread slide between shuttle and forefinger until it snaps off the back end of the shuttle. Notice that the thread glides easily between shuttle and finger, and there is no need to move the finger out of the way or to lift it from the shuttle. Without turning or twisting the shuttle, bring the thread back out between the bottom of the shuttle and the thumb (fig. 3-35). Again, there is no need to move the thumb. Stop in the position shown in Figure 3-36.

Here is the proper way to form the first half of the tatting knot: again take the position in Figure 3-33, and, turning the right hand palm up, secure the thread leading from the shuttle by folding the middle, ring, and little fingers down over the thread (fig. 3-37). Turn the right hand palm down, and point the shuttle under the thread that runs from the little finger of the right hand to the thumb and forefinger of the left (fig. 3-38). The shuttle thread is now out of the way over the backs of the right fingers. Take the shuttle under and back over the ring thread, without turning or twisting it, and it will automatically go through the loop (fig. 3-39). The shuttle always points in the same direction. Reverse the knot-bearer, slide the half hitch to the left, and begin the second half of the tatting knot.

This time there is no problem. The shuttle will go through the loop if taken directly over and then back under the ring thread. For this half of the knot, then, you do not run the shuttle thread over the backs of the fingers.

Variations on a theme, using the shuttle

Now let us go back and review all the figures made previously, this time using the shuttle. Although you are only going to vary the basic skills you have already learned, the use of a tool allows further variations on each of the basic steps.

The ring. The series of rings shown in Figure 3-40a was made with a basic ring of eight knots, with picots and joins at evenly spaced intervals. The first ring had six knots, a picot, then two more knots. The series can be carried on indefinitely by repeating the second ring to make the simplest of tatted edgings. Instructions for such an edging read:

Ring, 6 double stitches, picot, 2 double stitches, close.
*Space, ring, 2 double stitches, join to picot of last ring, 4 double stitches, picot, 2 double stitches, close. Repeat from * for desired length. Omit picot when making last ring.

Remember that the term *double stich* refers to the complete two-part knot. The direction, *picot*, means simply, "leave a space that will become a picot." The stitch that completes the picot is always included in the number given for the group of stitches that follow.

The simplest way to vary this pattern is by making more knots in each ring. The rings in Figure 3-40b have three times the number of knots in the smaller rings. For this series, follow the directions above, but wherever there is a group of double stitches, multiply the number given by three, and make that many knots. The length of thread left between the rings must be increased proportionately.

The rings may be of different sizes. In Figure 3-40c, the large and small rings of the first two patterns have been combined in a rhythmic repetition. The picot on the large ring has been lowered a bit also:

Ring, 20 double stitches, picot, 4 double stitches, close.
*(Space, 2 double stitches, join to picot of last ring, 4 double stitches, picot, 2 double stitches, close.) Repeat instructions in parentheses. Space, 4 double stitches, join to picot of last ring, 16 double stitches, picot, 4 double stitches, close. Repeat from * for desired length. Omit picot when making last ring.

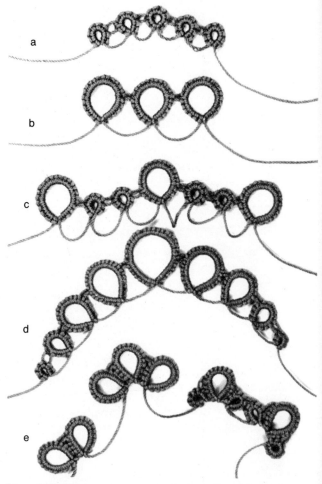

Figure 3-40. Five ways to vary a simple ring pattern. Included are small rings (a), large rings (b), small and large rings (c), graduated rings (d), and trefoil or cloverleaf arrangement (e).

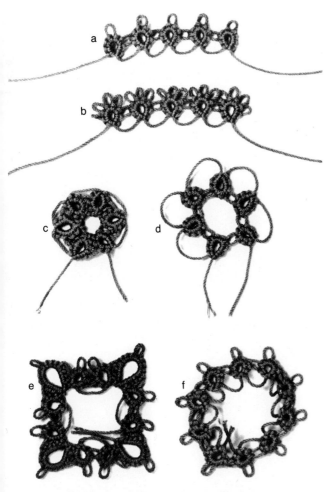

Figure 3-41. Six further variations by means of picots or joining patterns. Included are ornamental picots (a and b), circles with rings facing inward (c and d) or outward (f) and a square formed from trefoils (e).

One can also make a series of rings in graduated sizes, first increasing each successive ring by a constant number of knots, and then decreasing by the same number until the original size is again reached. In Figure 3-40d, each ring in the ascending series has eight more stitches than the preceding one, and in the descending series each has eight fewer stitches. These are distributed equally above and below the picots, except for the center ring where the picot was lowered somewhat. A series can also be made in which all the rings are of different sizes.

By eliminating the length of thread between rings, two- and three-ring clusters can be made. The rings in each cluster do not need to be all the same size (fig. 3-40e).

The picot. Adding ornamental picots makes a pattern look quite different. In Figure 3-41a, a picot has been added at the top of each ring:

Ring, 4 double stitches, 2 picots separated by 2 double stitches, 2 double stitches, close. *Space, ring, 2 double stitches, join to last picot of previous ring, 2 double stitches, 2 picots separated by 2 double stitches, 2 double stitches, close. Repeat from * for desired length. Omit last picot when making final ring.

In Figure 3-41b, picots have been added between all the knots above the place where the rings are joined:

Ring, 2 double stitches, 5 picots separated by 1 double stitch, 2 double stitches, close. *Space, ring, 2 double stitches, join to last picot of previous ring, 1 double stitch, 4 picots separated by 1 double stitch, 2 double stitches, close. Repeat from * for desired length.

The picots may be made long, short, or in a variety of sizes. In each case, the appearance of the pattern will be different.

Geometrical shapes. Circular shapes result when the first and last rings in a row of tatting are joined. The rings may lie with their tops out as in Figure 3-41f, or with them in toward the center, as in Figure 3-41d. In Figure 3-41c, a picot about twice the normal size was made at the top of the first ring, and all succeeding rings were joined to it. They were also joined at the sides, although they need not have been. Four clusters joined into a circle make a square (fig. 3-41e), and the square becomes a rectangle when more rings in equal numbers are added to two opposite sides.

The chain. A more radical change takes place when a chain is substituted for the length of thread between the rings (fig. 3-42a):

Use shuttle and ball of thread. Ring, 2 double stitches, 2 picots separated by 4 double stitches, 2 double stitches, close. *Reverse work, chain, 4 double stitches, picot, 4 double stitches. Reverse work, ring, 2 double stitches, join to last picot of previous ring, 4 double stitches, picot, 2 double stitches, close. Repeat from * for desired length.

Here again, many variations are possible. In addition, the chain may be of various lengths, and with or without picots. Beginning instructions for working with chains and rings are given on page 33.

Working with two shuttles. Finally, two shuttles come into play (fig. 3-42b; see also fig. 3-32c):

Two shuttles are required for this pattern. Ring, 2 double stitches, 2 picots separated by 4 double stitches, 2 double stitches, close. Reverse work, chain, 3 double stitches (i.e., work chain of 3 double stitches over thread wound on second shuttle). Change shuttles, ring, 2 double stitches, 2 picots separated by 4 double stitches, 2 double stitches, close. *Change shuttles. Chain, 3 double stitches. Reverse work, ring, 2 double stitches, join to last picot of next-to-last ring made, 4 double stitches, picot, 2 double stitches, close. Reverse work, chain, 3 double stitches. Change shuttles, ring, 2 double stitches, join to last picot of next-to-last ring made, 4 double stitches, picot, 2 double stitches, close. Repeat from * for desired length.

These patterns are only a few of the many designs that can be created with the basic ring, picot, and chain. More ideas for creating pattern units are given in Chapter 5, and suggestions for complete projects may be found in this chapter and Chapters 7 and 8.

Figure 3-42. Variations in patterns can be made by combining rings and chains. A simple pattern may be formed with a shuttle and ball thread (a); a more complicated pattern requires two active threads (b).

Odds and Ends

Abbreviations are almost always used in printed directions for tatting designs. They are fairly standard, although there are occasional slight variations. From now on in this book, all directions will be abbreviated. The key will also be found at the end of the book.

ch	chain
cl	close
ds	double stitch, double stitches
p	picot, picots
r	ring
rw	reverse work
sep	separated
sp	space

Ends are usually finished by tying them together in a square knot, and cutting them short. This is satisfactory when fine threads are used, but care should be taken to see that it is always done on the same side of the tatting. With cord as thick as the DMC size 3, ends should be avoided wherever possible. Those that cannot be eliminated should be tied, cut,

and also whipped to the wrong side of the work with needle and matching sewing cotton. This makes them virtually invisible. The ends of heavier thread and cord can be worked into the design as fringe, or hidden. Various methods for finishing off heavy contemporary tatted pieces are given in Chapter 4.

When using DMC size 3 or heavier crochet cotton, the last ring made may be reopened in order to correct mistakes. Do not try to open the ring all at once. Instead, reach in with the pick of the shuttle about two knots from the end, and pull up the knot-bearer (fig. 3-43). Move several knots to the left, and repeat. The thread is most easily pulled up where there is a picot, and after about the third pull (three picots) the ring will slide open all the way so that the knots can be undone one by one. Once you have undone the last ring, you can undo the one before it, and so on.

In fine work, cut away the error, leaving long ends for tying, and continue. When the work has progressed a little way, go back, tie, off, and clip. If a thread breaks, the same tying on procedure may be used with fine threads. However, splicing will be necessary for heavy threads. See the discussion of joining on page 69.

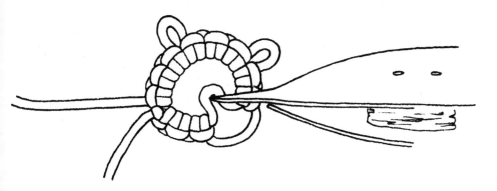

Figure 3-43. Opening a heavy ring to make corrections. Do not try to spread the ring apart at the bottom, since that makes the job more difficult. Instead, pull up the bearing thread at the picots.

Three projects

A tatting bag.   Figure 3-44 shows a little bag in filet crochet that dates from about 1915. It is a tatting bag, just large enough to hold a shuttle or two and a ball of tatting cotton. Like the knotting bag, its eighteenth-century counterpart, it was worn over the left wrist while working. For the fine work of those days, pins were often used for joining, and so a safety pin was fastened to the inside.

Figures 3-45 and 3-46 show tatted versions of the tatting bag and a knotting bag. They are made with size 3 crochet cotton. Complete instructions are given, not so they can be slavishly copied, but in order to allow the reader to see how tatted objects are put together, using only the techniques already covered in this chapter. The first shows how to combine rows of tatting to make a fabric, and the bottom of the second illustrates how to make a tatted circle.

Notice especially that patterns can be planned to fit together without sewing, and that such things as handles can be an integral part of the design. Having studied the bags, try to vary them to suit your own tastes, or, better still, devise something quite different. One suggestion is shown in Figure 3-47.

For those who have trouble getting started with their own designs, I suggest beginning with the flat bottom of the bag in Figure 3-46. Tat it through the third round, varying it a bit, even if only by the addition of a few picots. Instead of using it as a bottom, use it as a side. Then make another circle for the other side of the bag. This second side need not be exactly the same as the first, but it has to be the same size. Join the two circles with another round of tatting, leaving an opening at the top, and devise a handle. The result should be something like Figure 3-47. To save crochet cotton, use cotton parcel-post twine to work out your patterns. Once ready to begin on the bag itself, eliminate ends wherever possible, and overload the shuttle, within limits, so that joining is less frequent. If the openings in your bag are large enough for things to slip through, the bag should be lined.

Figure 3-44. Tatting bag in filet crochet, about 1915. The main part of the bag is about 4 inches square. (Courtesy of Bessie G. Murphy.)

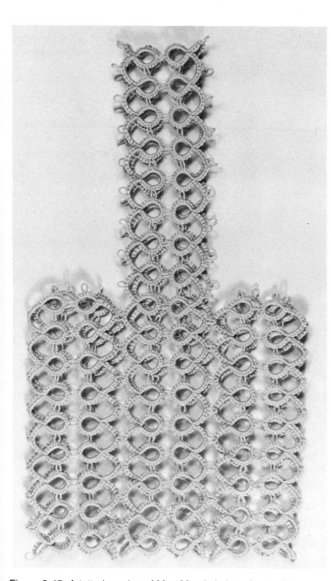

The bag in Figure 3-45 consists entirely of rows of tatting similar to the pattern in Figure 3-42a. The rows are connected alternately ring to ring and chain to chain. Two of the "rows" are actually rounds.

Use shuttle and ball of thread. First two rounds form handle and center of bag. *First round:* R, 5ds, 3p sep by 5ds, 5ds, cl. *Rw, ch, 5ds, p, 5ds. Rw, r, 5ds, join to last p of previous r, 5ds, 2p sep by 5ds, 5ds, cl. Repeat from * until 33 chains have been completed. Rw, r, 5ds, join to last p of previous r, 5ds, p, 5ds, join without twisting to first p of first r made, 5ds, cl. Rw, ch, 5ds, p, 5ds. Tie to base of first r. Cut and whip ends to wrong side. *Second round:* R, 5ds, p, 5ds, join to center p of any r in previous round, 5ds, p, 5ds, cl. *Rw, ch, 5ds, p, 5ds. Rw, r, 5ds, join to last p of previous r, 5ds, join to center p of next r in previous round, 5ds, p, 5ds, cl. Repeat from * around, joining last r as before and also joining it to first p of first r in round. Tie, cut, and whip ends. *First row of side:* R, 5ds, 3p sep by 5ds, 5ds, cl. Rw, ch, 5ds, join to p of any ch in either of first two rounds, 5ds. *Rw, r, 5ds, join to last p of previous r, 5ds, 2p sep by 5ds, 5ds, cl. Rw, ch, 5ds, join to p of next ch in previous round, 5ds. Repeat from * until 18 rings have been made. Tie, cut, and whip ends. *Second row of side:* R, 5ds, p, 5ds, join to central p of last r in first row of side, 5ds, p, 5ds, cl. *Rw, ch, 5ds, p, 5ds. Rw, r, 5ds, join to last p of previous r, 5ds, join to central p of next r in previous row, 5ds, p, 5ds, cl. Repeat from * until 10 rings have been made. Rw, ch, 5ds, join to p of eighth ch, 5ds. **Rw, r, 5ds, join to last p of previous r, 5ds, join to central p of next r in previous row, 5ds, p, 5ds, cl. Rw, ch, 5ds, join to p of next ch, 5ds. Repeat from ** to end of row, ending with r. Tie, cut, and whip ends. *Other side of bag:* Work in the same way. If desired, pull narrow ribbons vertically through some of the openings.

Figure 3-45. A tatted version of Mrs. Murphy's bag. Instructions are given here, which illustrate the simple principles of construction that can be used to form many tatted objects.

A drawstring knotting bag. The drawstring bag in Figure 3-46 begins with a rosette consisting of six rings. This is encircled by rounds of tatting, each with about twice as many rings as the last, until a flat circle five or six inches in diameter has been made. To bring the sides up vertically, keep the number of rings constant in succeeding rounds.

Rosette: R, 5ds, 3p sep by 5ds, 5ds, cl. *R, 5ds, join to last p of previous r, 5ds, 2p sep by 5ds, 5ds, cl. Repeat from * until there are 6 rings, joining last r as before and also joining it to first p of first r. Tie, cut, and whip ends. *Second round* (use shuttle and ball of thread): R, 5ds, p, 5ds, join to rosette at any point where two rings are joined, 5ds, p, 5ds, cl. *Rw, ch, 3ds, 2p sep by 4ds, 3ds. Rw, r, 5ds, join to last p of previous r, 5ds, join to next p of rosette, 5ds, p, 5ds, cl. Rw, ch, 3ds, 2p sep by 4ds, 3ds. Rw, r, 5ds, join to last p of previous r, 5ds, join to next junction of rings in rosette, 5ds, p, 5ds, cl. Repeat from * around, also joining last r to first. Tie and cut. *Third round* (use 2 shuttles): R, 5ds, p, 5ds, join to any p of previous round, 5ds, p, 5ds, cl. Rw, ch, 5ds. Change shuttles, r, 5ds, 3p sep by 5ds, 5ds, cl. Change shuttles, ch, 5ds. *Rw, r, 5ds, join to last p of next-to-last r made, 5ds, join to next p of last round, 5ds, p, 5ds, cl. Rw, ch, 5ds. Change shuttles, r, 5ds, join to last p of next-to-last r made, 5ds, 2 p sep by 5ds, 5ds, cl. Change shuttles, ch, 5ds. Repeat from * around, also joining last 2 rings to first 2. Tie and cut. *Fourth and fifth rounds* (use shuttle and ball of thread): Join to p of previous round, *ch, 5ds, p, 5ds, join to next p of previous round. Repeat from * around. Tie and cut. *Sixth through eleventh rounds:* Repeat third, fourth and fifth rounds twice more. *Twelfth round* (use shuttle and ball of thread): R, 5ds, 3p sep by 5ds, 5ds, cl. *(R, 5ds, join to last p of previous r, 5ds, 2p sep by 5ds, 5ds, cl) twice. Rw, ch, 10ds, join to p of previous round, 10ds. Rw, r, 5ds, p, 5ds, join to center p of last r, 5ds, p, 5ds, cl. Repeat from * around, joining center of last r to center p of first r made. Tie and cut. Pull ribbons through spaces between tenth and eleventh rounds. Decorate as desired.

An edging from the nineteenth century. This design, shown partially worked in Figure 3-48, is from Mrs. Pullan's book, published in 1853, which was discussed in the history of tatting. It is included here as a kind of introduction to the innovations suggested in Chapters 5 and 6, for this pattern from the past is hardly related to the way we tat today. The author suggested that it could be worked in fine or heavy thread, and she also included directions for narrower and wider variations. The unfamiliar instructions have been translated into modern terminology.

Wind shuttle. Tie free end of thread into eye of blunt-pointed tapestry needle. Begin work about a yard from needle, making all chains with needle and all rings with shuttle. Ch, 5ds, p, 6ds. Insert short length of heavy thread between needle and shuttle threads before making next knot. (This takes the place of a picot on the needle thread called for in the original instructions, but which pulls out and disappears far too easily.) Ch, 5ds. R, 5ds, join to p, 14ds, p, 5ds, cl. Ch, 5ds, insert another short length of thread, 5ds. R, 5ds, join to p of last r made, 14ds, p, 5ds, cl. *Ch, 3ds. R, 5ds, join to p of last r made, 14ds, p, 4ds, cl. Ch, 3ds. R, 4ds, join to p of last r made, 16ds, p, 4ds, cl. Ch, 3ds. R, 4ds, join to p of last r made, 14ds, p, 5ds, cl. Ch, 3ds. R, 5ds, join to p of last r made, 7ds, 2p sep by 7ds, 5ds, cl. Ch, 5ds, join to ch where second thread was inserted (pass needle through), 5ds. R, 5ds, join to last p of previous r, 7ds, 2p sep by 7ds, 5ds, cl. Ch, 5ds, join to ch where first thread was inserted, 6ds, join to last p of previous r, 10ds, p, 6ds, insert thread, 5ds. R, 5ds, join to p of ch, 7ds, join to central p of last r in cluster just completed, 7ds, p, 5ds, cl. Ch, 5ds, insert thread, 5ds. R, 5ds, join to last p of previous r, 7ds, join to central p of next-to-last r in cluster just completed, 7ds, p, 5ds, cl. Repeat from * until desired number of clusters has been made, ending ch, 5ds instead of ch, 10ds. If either thread runs out, tie on a new piece. *For wider edging:* Repeat second r and ch that precedes it, and sixth r and ch that follows it, any number of times. *For narrower edging:* Omit these same sections entirely.

Figure 3-48 shows edging in progress with wide version in the middle and narrow version at bottom. Note that the short lengths of thread inserted for holding picots are shown in the edging at top.

Figure 3-48. A nineteenth-century edging pattern by Mrs. Pullan, worked in three variations. A pattern is given for the top variation, which is shown in progress.

Figure 3-46. A small tatted version of the eighteenth-century knotting bag. Instructions are given.

Figure 3-47. Another suggestion for a tatted bag. Study how it is made, and then vary it, or better still, devise your own version.

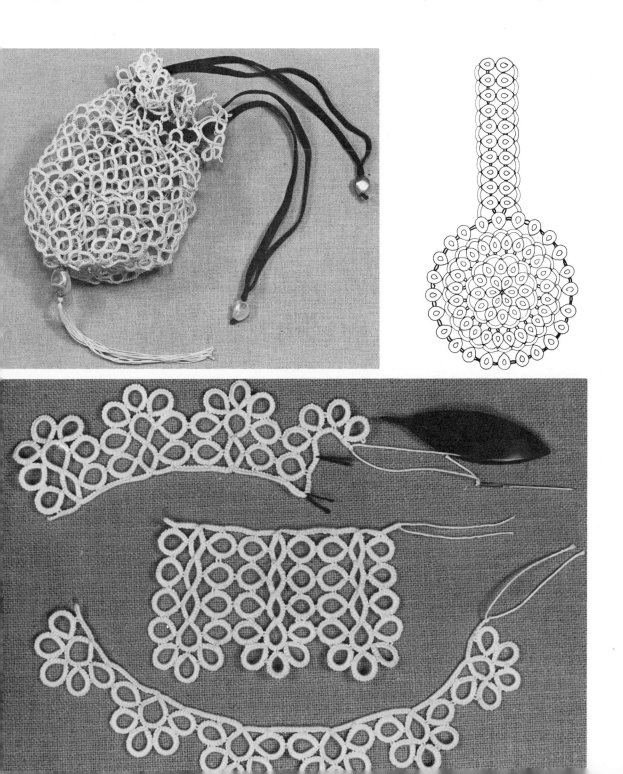

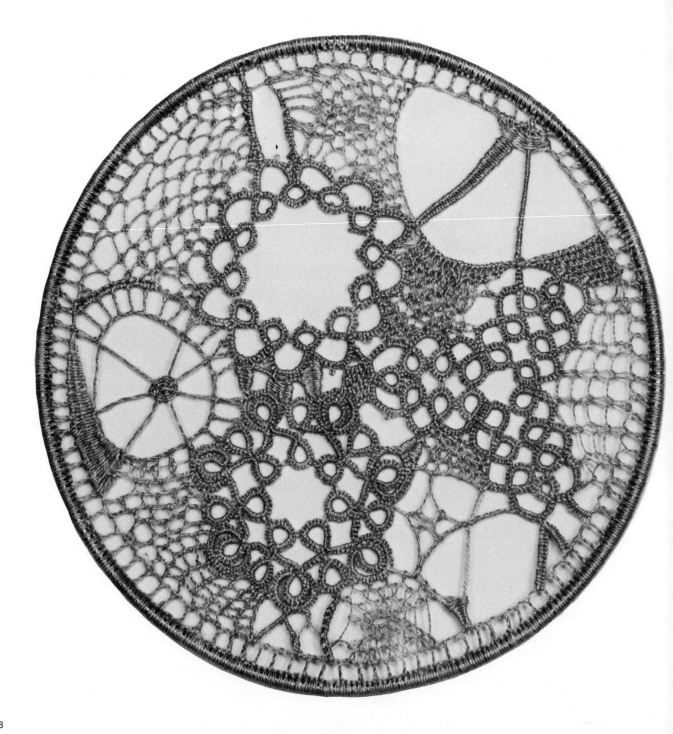

4 / New Ways

Tools and Materials for Contemporary Work

Traditional tatting tools, described in Chapter 2, were devised during a time when people used finer thread for tatting. A sufficient length of today's thicker tatting materials will hardly fit in the shuttles now sold or even in the somewhat larger traditional shuttles, devised for decorating furnishing fabrics. The second-hand market sometimes yields these larger, three-to-five-inch shuttles, but even they have only limited use. The answer seems to be to improvise.

Figure 4-1. Contemporary materials open a whole new world to the tatter. This circular form in linen thread combines tatting, needlepoint-lace stitches, and needleweaving. The stitches are supported by a metal ring covered with buttonholing. (Courtesy of Mieke Kerkstra.)

Figure 4-2. Simple but effective shuttle substitute is tightly rolled ball secured with rubber band. Shuttles are just too small to hold a sufficient length of the heavier threads used in contemporary tatting, such as the cotton cable twist shown here. The ball must be small enough to pass through the ring thread.

Figure 4-3. The yarn-bobbin shape has been used in the past for creating effective tatting tools that hold long lengths of yarn. *Above*: shuttle used by Lady Hoare's mother in late nineteenth-century England; *below*: Scandanavian shuttle.

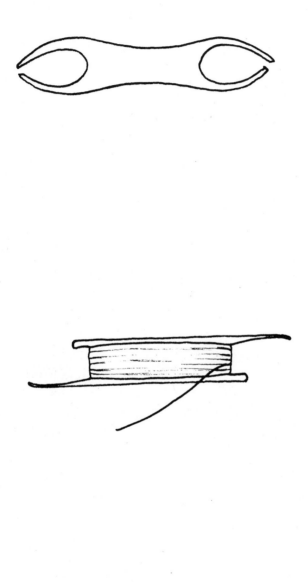

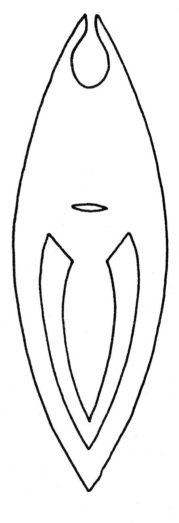

Figure 4-4. A very satisfactory tatting shuttle, a variation of a netting shuttle, can be cut from a plastic bottle or sheet. Trace the pattern right from the book, as it is reproduced same size.

Improvising tools

The choice of shuttle substitute depends not only on personal preference, but on the kind of thread being used. Smooth materials can be rolled into balls and secured with tight rubber bands as in Figure 4-2. The balls roll easily over the ring thread, making it possible to go very fast, and, with practice, quite large ones can be manipulated. However, the rubber bands must fit snugly or they will work themselves off and fly across the room. This method is perhaps the most satisfactory of those outlined here. Try it with cotton parcel-post twine, beginning with about twelve yards per ball.

If the thread is fuzzy, like knitting yarn, rubber bands will strip off the fuzz, and the simplest solution is to use yarn bobbins, jumbo size (see fig. 2-11). These are sold as tools for bulky knitting yarns, and therefore they hold extremely long lengths of any thinner yarn. Even when practice has shown you the best way to manipulate them, you will find them, because of their length, to be considerably more clumsy than the balls secured with rubber bands, and they will never allow you to work quite as fast. As mentioned before, people with large hands might like to try the shorter, wider version that is also made. The regular-sized bobbins previously described (see fig. 2-4) handle easily and are useful when very long lengths of relatively fine thread are being used. Because these smaller bobbins are made from plastic that is quite thin, it is often more satisfactory to wind the thread on two which have been placed together. Interestingly, there is historical precedent for tools of this general yarn-bobbin shape (fig. 4-3).

Homemade shuttles can be tailored to individual needs and preferences in more than one way. Figure 4-4 is a drawing of a shuttle offered for sale by a thread manufacturer in 1917. Really nothing more than a shorter, rounder version of a netting shuttle, it is perfectly flat and may be cut from a large plastic bottle. Modify the resulting plastic pattern until you find the ideal size and shape (the original shuttle was for fine thread and was much smaller). Then substitute some more permanent material, such as wood, and craft an improvised shuttle from it with the aid of the plastic template. To wind this shuttle, catch the end of the thread in the slit, take it around the central tongue, and then carry it to the other side by way of the bottom, again slipping it behind the central tongue. Continue in this fashion, constantly going from one side to the other (fig. 4-5). Unless wound in this way, the tool holds very little thread.

Figure 4-5. Proper way to wind this shuttle.

Figure 4-6. A homemade acrylic shuttle. The center post, which is glued in, should be as long and narrow as possible, while still keeping within practical dimensions, so that the shuttle will hold a maximum amount of thread. (Courtesy of Susan E. Munstedt.)

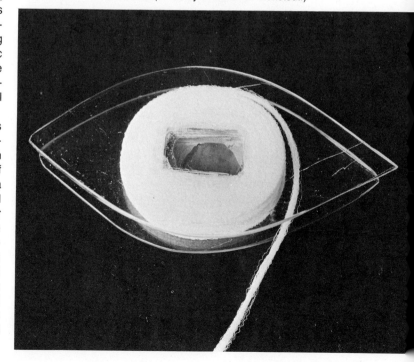

Another homemade shuttle is shown in Figure 4-6. It is made from acrylic, which can be cut with an ordinary pocket knife. Acrylic sheets about one-eighth inch thick (Lucite or similar material), along with a special adhesive, are available where art supplies are sold.

Part of the problem in using any shuttle is that the span of the fingers of the left hand,which holds the ring thread open, limits the size of the tool that can pass through. A homemade version of the Victorian sewing bird often improves matters greatly, especially when tatting large rings or using heavy cord. To make it, mount a spring clothespin anywhere that is convenient. The one pictured in Figure 4-7, which is on a stand fashioned from a length of dowel and a board, is portable. Be sure to sand the "jaws" of the clothespin smooth, so that they will not catch and damage the thread, or line them with glued-in oblongs of felt. The clothespin takes the place of the middle finger of the left hand, and holds the ring open wide enough for large balls of yarn to pass through.

Other tools may be needed from time to time as aids in closing rings or pulling knots shut, depending on the friction a material creates. A pair of long, round-nosed pliers, of the sort used in basketry, can sometimes be very helpful. From now on in this book, the term *shuttle* refers either to the shuttle or its substitute.

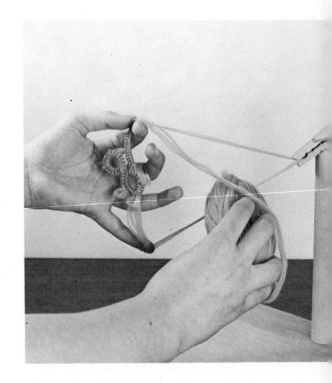

Figure 4-7. A homemade version of a sewing bird, which serves as a substitute for the position of the left hand in tatting, the one that holds the ring thread.

Figure 4-8. Mobiles made from experimental tatted pieces make excellent projects for beginners. Here heavy pearl cotton, knitting worsted, various kinds of viscose straw, and medium-weight satin cord have been used. (Courtesy of Vivian Poon.)

Threads, yarns, cords, and twines

Today there is a wide range of threads available to the craftsman. Shops catering to weavers seem to be springing up everywhere, and craft and hobby shops stock increasingly large supplies of materials for macramé, many of which can be used for tatting. Knit shops, variety stores, department stores, hardware stores, and sporting goods shops all carry threads and cords of one kind or another. Which of these materials are suitable for tatting? Obviously, unless the work is to be limited to chains, something strong enough to withstand the tugging when rings are pulled shut is needed. Nor can rings be closed if they are made of textured or bumpy materials. Such thread would detract in any case, from the special appearance of tatting, which has a texture of its own. Also to be avoided is anything that has much tendency to twist or untwist as you work with it. Very elastic materials will not do, but 4-ply knitting yarn and rug yarn, both of which have a certain amount of elasticity, do very nicely.

The criterion, then, seems to be whether or not a ring made with the thread being tested can be closed. But do not interpret the rule too narrowly. Some materials will not make large rings satisfactorily, but are fine for small ones, which means only that, in working with them, there will be a more limited choice of design. And even this deficiency can be overcome by including large mock rings formed by pushing the knots on a chain close together and tying or otherwise fastening them into a circle. A thread that will not work by itself may do nicely in chains, as the ball thread, when cotton is used in the shuttle (or its substitute). This technique has been resorted to since the last century to allow the use of rather inflexible gold or silver thread.

Some nylon presents special problems because more than ordinary strength is needed to pull the rings shut. Nylon stitching twine, a 3-cord nylon thread about the size of crochet cotton size 20, and which appears to be waxed, almost falls into this category, and very large rings made with it are difficult to close perfectly. Nylon mason line defies all ordinary pulling and pliers must be used; even then it is necessary to pull very hard. Mason line is cord used by stone masons, and is carried by hardware stores. It is yellow, although it sometimes comes in green. Not everyone will be willing or even able to work with this difficult-to-use cord, but for those who are, the results are well worth it. The belt illustrated in Figure 4-9 was made in a couple of evenings and is outstanding for its beautiful gold color and rich texture.

Tying ends may be a problem if certain other threads are chosen, particularly rayon. Although the material often gives no difficulty at all when tatting with it, tying the finishing knot may resist all one's efforts since knots made with this material have an irritating tendency to undo themselves. The solution is to sew the knot with needle and cotton sewing thread, or to put a drop of glue or clear nail polish on it. In the latter case, if the piece is to be washed or cleaned, something must be chosen that will not be removed in the process. Nylon is also sometimes difficult to tie, but, since nylon melts, the ends can often be fused by burning. Be careful to do this inconspicuously or a discolored spot may result. And a warning must be added: be sure it is *nylon* you have in hand before lighting the match. Some synthetics are highly flammable.

Those who want to incorporate metallic threads into their work will find a number to choose from. As noted above, the technical problem that some of them present, that of being too stiff, is easily taken care of by using them for chains while working with cotton or other, more flexible thread in the shuttle. However, they are difficult to use for another reason. As those who have tried them for embroidery know, they can be quite satisfactory for flat stitches like satin stitch, which reflects the light back evenly and uniformly, but when they are worked in twisted or knotted stitches, they often tend to become either dull-looking or cheap and tinselly. Since tatting is knotted, many metallic threads simply cannot be used for it. This does not mean that threads of this sort are not to be used for tatting. However, their limitations must be explored, and certainly no large supply of any one thread should be laid in before experimenting carefully. Some yarn companies carry a line of thin wool plied with metallic thread, which is very flexible.

Probably the best choice of thread for early projects and general use is Lily Double-Quick, a cotton cable twist which is inexpensive, easy to handle, and results in a good-looking, durable product. Few other blanket recommendations can be made, since something that one person enjoys using may drive someone else straight up the wall. Satin cord, which comes in more than one thickness, will suit most people, but jute and plastic clothesline are decidedly in the difficult-to-use category. Some materials hold surprises. Viscose straw makes the same size ring if it is split in two, but handles easier and goes further. Incidentally, it is especially attractive if placed with another kind of thread, such as propylene knitting yarn, and the two worked as though they were one.

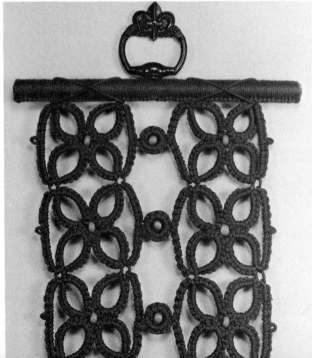

Figure 4-9. Girdle (belt) of yellow nylon mason line. The fringe is decorated with bullion knots, described in Chapter 9. (Courtesy of Tom Paddock.)

Figure 4-10. Detail of wall hanging of cotton cable twist with ceramic beads. The thread, which is easy to handle and results in a crisp, tailored look, is especially recommended to those who teach beginners or children. (See detail of lower half, fig. 8-13.)

Figure 4-11. Tatting on a grand scale, shown against a tree for size. This tatted hanging was made from green and white plastic clothesline. (Courtesy of Caroline Hunkel Kitelinger.)

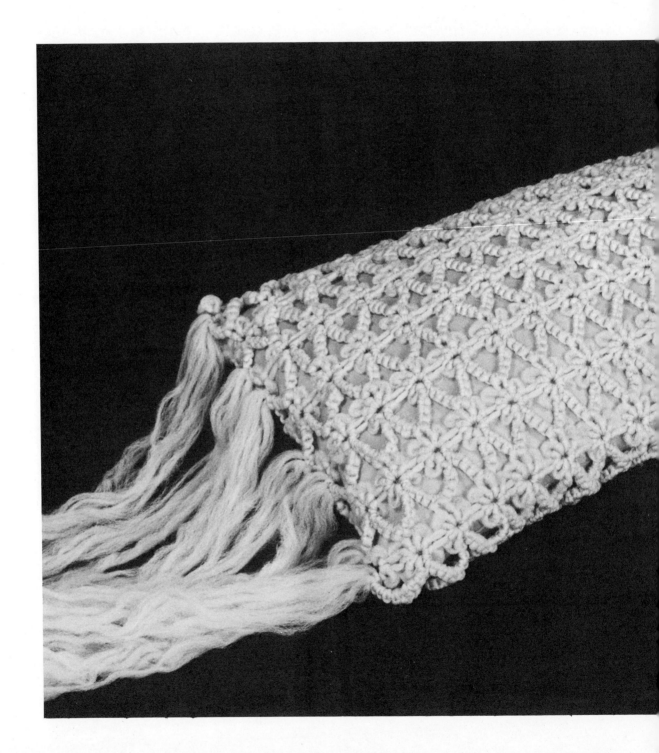

Making swatches. The threads and cords mentioned above are not the only choices. Experiment by making tatted swatches with everything that comes to hand that looks at all suitable. Do not reject a thread simply because it does not work up well in a particular pattern; not all threads take to every design. About the only generalization that can be made is that heavy materials tend to look better if worked into simple rather than elaborate configurations. The material in Chapter 5 will provide a springboard for experimentation. The only rule is: Never throw away a sample. An idea that is a total failure in one thread can be a triumphant success in another, and a combination of thread and pattern that is too soft in one situation may do nicely somewhere else with just a little adjustment. Also, unsuccessful trials, if they are put aside for a while and not thought about consciously, frequently lead to new ideas, or can be made workable.

Remember that the use to which the item will be put, as well as the appearance, must be taken into account. A seat cover or a tote bag should stand up under friction and resist soil, while a wall hanging need not. For that reason, nylon, linen, or hardwearing wool should be chosen for the former, but probably not cotton. Likewise, something too soft for a belt may be just the thing for a vest, or a relatively stretchy fabric may be useful where expandability is desirable, but not where structural rigidity is called for.

Figure 4-12. Cushion of polypropylene knitting yarn. The inner cushion cover is broadcloth. When a colorful backing is used, as here with orange cloth under yellow yarn, the see-through effect of tatting can be very attractive.

Estimating Length. Every project should begin with a working sampler, or a series of experiments, worked until the right combination of thread and pattern is found. The resulting swatch is very important both for determining how much material will be needed for the total project and for keeping an exact record of your experiments. The easiest way to keep track of such swatches is to store them, labeled, in a deep box with a slot cut in the top. The label from the thread itself can be stapled to the sample, and you can write in any pertinent information that may be lacking: price, where the thread can be bought, other colors available, and — even more important — the length of thread used for the sample. This may be figured simply, by subtracting the length left on the shuttle from the total length you originally wound on to it. If the sample was made with a double shuttle, remember to calculate the lengths of both threads used.

The advantage of keeping swatches this way is that it allows unsystematic people to be systematic with the least amount of effort. More highly organized readers will no doubt have their own perhaps more elaborate ideas for record keeping.

Because of the difficulty in adding on lengths of cord, particularly when thick materials are used, good craftsmanship demands that such joins be avoided by working with an unbroken length of thread whenever possible. This means that the full length of thread must be wound onto the shuttle before beginning. There is no one formula to help determine length of thread or cord needed. Each pattern has different requirements, and, furthermore, when working with two or more shuttles, the requirements may be entirely different for each. Remember that the same thread does not have to be wound on each shuttle. There can be very different length requirements when more rings are made with one shuttle than the other or where the bearing thread does not switch back and forth from one shuttle to the other. The bearing thread uses up less length of cord than the thread that forms the knots.

If you have previously made a sample swatch of known length in the material and pattern, you can find the approximate length of cord for the total piece by simple multiplication. For example, if the sample was one ring and the finished piece needs 20 rings, you merely have to multiply the length of thread used in the sample by 20. In practice you may actually need a greater length than you have calculated, so leave a generous margin for error. When working in identical rows as for the pillow in Figure 4-12, closer estimates can be made after one row has been finished.

Ends and what to do with them

As we have seen, fine tatting is finished by tying the ends together in a square knot on the wrong side of the work, a generally impractical solution when heavier materials are used. Most of the time, in contemporary work, the easiest and best way is to plan each piece so that the ends are simply left as fringe. But when fringe absolutely will not do, another answer must be found.

Sometimes it is easy to draw an unwanted end through the knots in a ring or chain with the help of a tapestry needle or crochet hook. More likely, it will be difficult, and, on occasion, it is impossible. Therefore, before making your piece, be sure to test this method of finishing on a small sample of the particular thread. This is especially important when planning something that will be viewed from both sides.

Another possibility is whipping the ends, with needle and matching sewing thread, firmly to the wrong side of the work, just as recommended for size 3 crochet cotton. When making something without a wrong side — a room divider, perhaps — it may be possible to work the ends into a finishing row of crochet, buttonholing, or some sort of binding. Lined objects afford opportunities to hide ends in seams, although this must be done in such a way that there are no unwanted bumps or lumps. While many solutions are possible, planning ahead is essential, with consideration being given to where the ends will be at the finish, and with an idea or two in mind as to how to deal with them.

If the ends are to occur somewhere in the middle of a piece, they may be avoided by using a different method of construction. You have already seen how ends can be avoided, at the beginning of a piece, by starting at the center of a continuous thread (see page 43). Consider, also, a circular or oval piece consisting of several rounds of tatting. If you do not want to work this spiral fashion — spirals make tying off at the end of every round unnecessary — it is still possible to continue with an unbroken thread after completing each round. Instead of cutting and tying off the work at the end of a round, leave a length of thread unworked that is long and slack enough to be hidden, after the next round is begun, by whipping to the back of the work with needle and sewing cotton.

The tatting bag on page 55 illustrates how to construct a piece where several rows of tatting are joined together, and the knotting bag on page 56 demonstrates, in the construction of the bottom, how to join rounds when making a circle.

When joining is necessary, either when breaks occur because the work had to be ripped, or because thread ran out prematurely, tying on may be done, if the knot can be camouflaged in some way. Fringe or tassels added afterwards may be the best solution.

You may have to resort to splicing. Splicing is a method of attaching two cords without a knot. There are several methods. Choose by experimenting with what works best for the particular material you are using. Sometimes the strands of each end of the cord can be unraveled, about half of the strands of each cut away to reduce bulk, and the remainder intermeshed. The intermeshed strands are then fastened with one of the fabric glues on the market. For additional strength, it may also be necessary to secure the join by whipping or sewing with fine cotton. A ring cannot be made with a spliced cord, as it is impossible not to put too much tension on the splice when closing the ring. Such spliced joins should be used in chains only, even though it may be necessary to unravel some work in order to do so.

In general, the DMC size 3 thread can be tied, cut, and ends whipped to the reverse side of the work when joining is required. Anything finer should merely be tied and cut. Splicing is really only necessary when using quite bulky materials.

Trimmings and finishings

Contemporary tatting is not limited by traditional examples, so that decoration and finishing may encompass a wide range of imaginative materials. For instance, you might combine tatting with other needle crafts or with other art media. Instead of using tatting as a two-dimensional fabric, edging, or appliqué, you might mount it in reed or metal hoops, as shown in Figures 4-1 and 6-19, or create a soft sculpture. Small tatted pieces can be stiffened in plastic dipping solutions, and used in a number of ways.

Whatever trimming or finishing materials you choose, remember that they should suit both the purpose and the construction of the tatting itself. The rest is up to you. There are many suggestions for finished projects and their variations in the chapters that follow, but there are no fixed answers to the creative problems of contemporary tatting.

Figure 5-1. Josephine picot. This ring of half hitches is an ornament only for a chain.

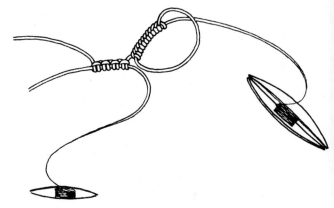

Figure 5-2. Josephine picots and Josephine knots. Complete Josephine picots ornament chains (a), rings are separated by a length of thread ornamented with a Josephine knot (b).

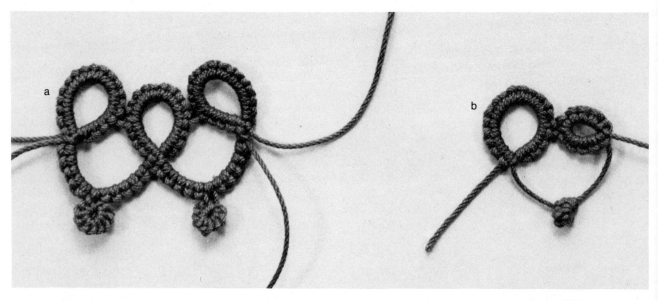

5/Getting Down to Basics

Design and Color

With the basic skills and techniques you have learned, you are now ready to design your own pieces. The versatility of tatting is not in the stitch units, since the double stitch is the only knot commonly used. There are some others that can be added for variety, though, such as the Josephine knot and picot (see below) and variations on the traditional knotting techniques described in Chapter 9. Instead, the creative potential of tatting lies in the variability of the pattern unit. Look again at some of the historical pieces in Chapter 1. All the intricate, lacy patterns were created by combining basic ring and chain formations in different ways. With contemporary yarns and colors, such patterns can produce a great wealth of designs.

This chapter explores some of the basic tatting formations that can be used as pattern units, as well as ideas for making the most of materials and color. It would be a good idea to read all of the different sections before starting on a design because a successfully planned piece must blend all the factors — pattern, shape, color, texture — into a harmonious whole.

Figure 5-3. Experimental piece with liberal use of bullion knots. (Courtesy Tom Paddock.)

Josephine picot and other knots

Most of the books on tatting published in this century included directions for making the Josephine picot even though this ornament is virtually never seen. It consists of a ring of four to twelve half knots, that is, half hitches. Such a device can only ornament a chain. It cannot be made within an ordinary ring, like a picot, because it has to be drawn closed separately. It is a purely decorative picot. To give it more stability, and counteract the twisting tendency of the half knots, the shuttle may be passed once through the ring thread, from front to back, before the Josephine picot is drawn up. Figure 5–1 shows a partially made Josephine picot. A pretty device, this can give tatting an unusual look, and warrants study (fig. 5-2a; see fig. 9-7a).

The *Dictionary of Needlework* by Caulfeild and Saward, describes instead the Josephine knot (fig. 5-2b). Made exactly like the Josephine picot, and probably its forerunner, it is used on the length of thread that separates two rings, when working with only one shuttle. In drawing it up, the goal is not to obtain a flat ring, but rather a thick lump, a fact which clearly shows it to be a survival of knotting.

In the nineteenth century, the first half of the knot used alone to form rings was known variously as half stitch, single stitch, or French stitch. The second half used alone to form rings was known as English stitch. However, both halves are needed to prevent twisting, and rings made entirely of either French or English stitch have a built-in twist just like Josephine picots.

Bullion knots (fig. 5-3, see fig. 9-3e), which ornament unknotted lengths of cord, are created simply by making a ring and winding the shuttle four times over the ring thread before closing it.

Design building blocks

The material in this section does not pretend to be an exhaustive catalog of basic tatting formations. It is intended as a starting point for ideas, and should be supplemented both with the forms that emerge from studying it, and with designs found elsewhere. Since contemporary threads generally lend themselves best to less elaborate configurations, those are the ones stressed. Asymmetrical patterns have not been included because you can develop them from the symmetrical patterns. Remember that the ideas set out below can be varied in all the ways discussed in Chapter 3: geometric shapes, picots, various sized rings, etc. In addition, if two shuttles are used, extra rings or Josephine picots can be added to any chain.

1. *Connected rings* (fig. 5-4). This pattern, with several variations, was covered in Chapter 3 (see figs. 3-32, 3-40).
2. *Cloverleafs* (fig. 5-5). The rings that make up the cloverleaf are generally attached to each other, and the last ring of each motif is usually attached also to the first ring of the next. However, other joinings are possible, and there is no need to limit the basic unit to three rings (see fig. 3-40e).
3. *Rings within rings* (fig. 5-6). The double ring can form the basis of exceptionally handsome designs. To make it, construct the inner ring in the usual way, making a picot at

its top. When this ring has been closed, begin a second, larger one, up close to it. No hard and fast rule can be given for the size of this second ring, but, in general, if there is to be any space between it and the inner ring, it must have at least three times the number of knots. When half of this second ring has been made, position the first ring within it and join them by pulling the ring thread of the outer ring up through the picot and putting the shuttle through the loop. Be sure it is the ring thread that is pulled up through the picot and not the shuttle thread, or the second ring will not close properly. If the outer ring needs to be very large, it may prove better to make a chain instead of a ring and to tie it at the bottom. If a nest of three rings is wanted, it is almost always necessary to make the outermost ring a chain. Picots may be supplied on the outer ring for joining to other rings as desired, and ornamental ones can be made anywhere.

4. *Ring clusters, type a* (fig. 5-7). Here the rings are joined together with their bases facing out, and, in order to get from one ring to another without tying off the work, a length of thread must be left or a chain made. If only three or four rings are involved, they may be joined together at their tops only by means of a single large picot made in the first ring. If more rings are involved, they must also be joined at their sides (see fig. 3-41c) unless overlapping is wanted. When making rows of such clusters in a straight line, they are worked in two journeys, a forward and return row.
5. *Ring clusters, type b* (fig. 5-8). If clusters are made with rings whose bases face in, no thread lengths or chains are needed between them, although, if desired, they may be included in circles consisting of many rings. If included, these connecting threads will fall inside the circle instead of framing it as in type a (see fig. 3-41f).
6. *Long clusters* (fig. 5-9). They may be worked with the rings facing in or out, and they may be made up of several rows of tatting.
7. *Chain formations* (fig. 5-10). Many open patterns can be tatted using nothing but chains, and, in addition, relatively solid areas can be achieved, something that is otherwise difficult to do in tatting. However, such dense areas made with chains are slow and tedious to work, since it takes many rows for a small piece of work.
8. *Miscellaneous configurations* (fig. 5-11). In addition to those shown, many other patterns can be devised. Try it and see. Be sure to plan ahead, so you know exactly where the connecting picots must fall.

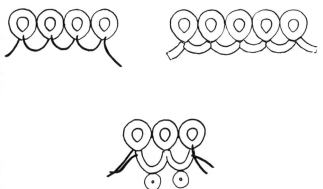

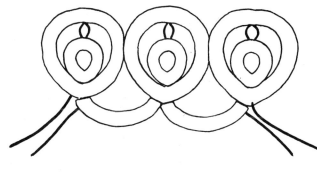

Figure 5-4. Connected rings. One of the most widely used tatting motifs combines rings or rings and chains in various ways.

Figure 5-6. Rings within rings. In general, the outer ring must have at least three times the number of knots as the inner ring.

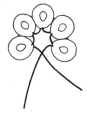 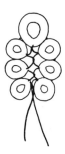

Figure 5-5. Cloverleafs. There is no need to limit this variation to a three-ring unit.

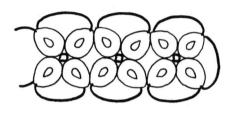
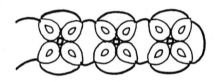

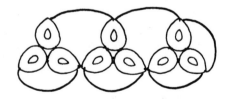
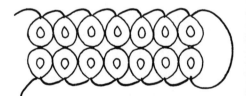

Figure 5-7. Ring clusters (type a) with their bases facing outward.

Figure 5-8. Ring clusters (type b) with their bases facing inward.

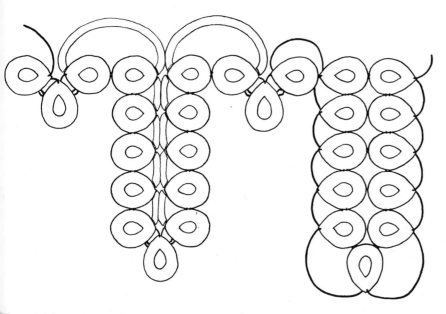

Figure 5-9. Long clusters. These can be made with rings facing in
or out, and can be varied with chains.

Figure 5-10. Chain formations. When chains are used alone, instead of as an adjunct to rings, interesting solid forms can result.

Figure 5-11. Miscellaneous formations. There is really no limit to the patterns that can be created with an imaginative use of the basic elements.

Fig. 5-12

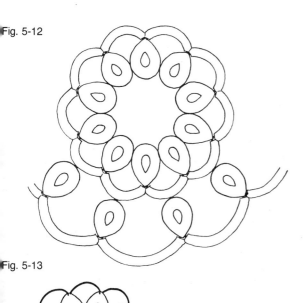

Fig. 5-13

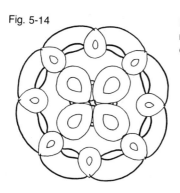

Fig. 5-14

Fig. 5-15

Composite circular motifs

Following are some of the most common beginnings for tatted circles. Larger circles are formed by continuing to add new rounds, as desired, in the same way. If the growing circle is to be kept flat, each successive ring must contain longer chains, more or larger rings than the last, or both. Otherwise the shape will draw in, resulting in a concave piece. Concave or convex shapes are useful in three-dimensional work, which is described in Chapter 6. Much of the material in this section can also be worked in straight lines, rather than in rounds, and the straight lines can be joined to form squares, rectangles, or other polygons (see fig. 5-20).

1. *Two rounds, bases facing out,* consisting of rings and usually joined together at the sides (fig. 5-12).

2. *Central ring with many picots, surrounded by a row of rings,* which are joined to each other at the sides and to the picots of the central ring at the top (fig. 5-13).

3. *Quatrefoil encircled by rings* (fig. 5-14). The inside unit is made with bases pointing inward, while the outside round is made with the bases out.

4. *Central ring with many picots, surrounded by qua-trefoils* (fig. 5-15).

5. *Central ring with many picots, surrounded by a row of rings,* which are placed one up and one down (fig. 5-16).

Figures 5-12, 5-13, 5-14, 5-15, and 5-16. Composite circular motifs. See if you can identify any of these in the historical examples in Chapter 1.

Fig. 5-16

Figures 5-17, 5-18, 5-19, and 5-20. Building geometric shapes. Angles can be created by a three-ring unit in which the center ring is larger than the other two. On a larger scale, angles can be formed by the placement of rows of tatting.

Geometric shapes

1. *Basic geometric shapes* such as squares, triangles, and ovals may be built from circles (fig. 5-17). Where there are corners, they must be formed by making a larger ring where the angle is to be. If all the rings in the outside round are the same size, a rounded shape will result. The inside units shown here are the same as that in Figure 5-12, but any basic motif may be substituted.

2. *Squares, hexagons,* etc., without inner circles, may be formed in the same way, by alternating large rings or chains with small ones (fig. 5-18).

3. *Ovals or rectangles* can be built by continuing around, in a spiral or coil fashion, after completing a single or double row of tatting. Large rectangular or square shapes can be made by this same principle. However, where there are corners, rings at the corners must be larger than the others in every round (fig. 5-19).

4. *Straight lines with scalloped edges* can be formed from a series of round motifs. Small square or circular motifs can be built up from such compound straight lines to form large areas, although both these forms should be avoided when heavy thread or cord is used since too many ends are produced (fig. 5-20).

Fig. 5-17

Fig. 5-18

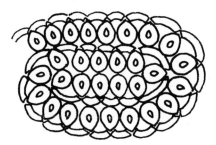

Fig. 5-19

Fig. 5-20

Pattern and texture

Because tatting is formed of knots, it has a rich textural quality no matter what arrangement of knots is chosen or what threads are used. With so many patterns or arrangements of knots possible, and with so many kinds of material available, the problem in tatting is not to produce texture, but rather to use it effectively.

Two dangers are present whenever working in a technique that offers a wide range of textures. One stems from the erroneous idea that all textures are compatible. They are not. Texture, in this sense, is produced by a combination of thread and pattern. Similar textures will usually go together, but other combinations, such as a coarse with a fine texture, must be chosen with care.

The second misconception is that the more textures there are the better the design will be. If the finished piece is to show the simplicity and unity characteristic of an outstanding design, then one texture must predominate, and the others subordinate themselves to it. One of the easiest ways to produce a dominant texture is by merely using more of it.

When mistakes in texture balancing occur, what has probably been forgotten is that texture is subject to the same rules that apply to color or other design elements. As colors must be compatible, or clash for a good reason, so must textures; as colors must show dominance, subordination, and balance, so must textures. Different design elements must balance, too. If a piece has many colors, then it is unlikely that it ought to have many textures, and vice versa.

Density is another element of pattern that is closely related to texture. In tatting, designs can range from very open ones to those of medium density, as you have already seen. Yet, really solid areas are difficult to achieve, even though they may be necessary to the design. Chains can be used to build a solid area (see fig. 5-10), and overlapping of openwork rows can also produce a dense effect (fig. 5-21). But both these methods are tedious and slow. A far better solution is to combine tatting with other techniques, such as crochet, that can easily create dense areas of work with the same thread. An intermedia solution would be to include actual solid objects in the tatting. Large beads, or ceramic or metal plates with holes punched along the sides for attaching the threads, are only some of the possible solutions.

Proportion of dense to open areas is also important. The best tatted designs subordinate one to the other, and, unless this is done, it is easy to make monotonous patterns with almost no center of interest.

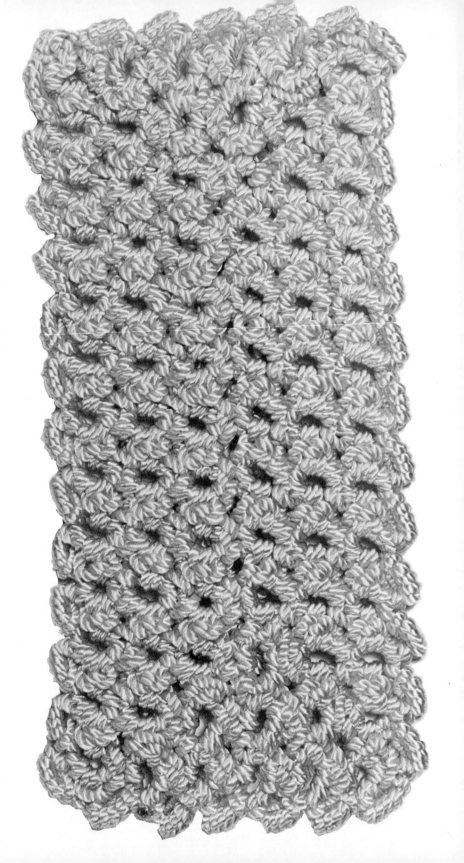

Color

Color is an important feature of modern textiles. Older tatting, if it used color at all, tended to use one color throughout, or if two colors were used, to wind the shuttle with one and to use the other from the ball or wind it on a second shuttle, depending on what kind of pattern was being worked. If you have practiced with different colors as already suggested, you know how colors distribute themselves naturally when separated in rings and chains. As previously described, you can make rings with one shuttle, chains with shuttle and ball of thread, and must use two shuttles if rings are to be positioned on the chains.

Be careful not to produce a design that has colors in about equal amounts, unless that effect is particularly desired. If one color is to form the chains and one the rings, or if the rings are different colors, as possible with two shuttles, you can estimate beforehand about how much of each color will appear in the final piece. Even in an equal distribution, one color can be made to predominate if the shade chosen is much brighter than the other color.

More flexibility can be achieved, even when using very heavy materials, if the threads are switched before a ring or chain is begun. If the chains are light and the rings dark, vary the pattern by making some of the chains dark and some of the rings light. Two active shuttle threads must be used, because a thread attached to a large ball will not pass through the ring thread, as it must when the color is switched. This method distorts the shape of the chain very slightly where the switch is made. The threads should always be crossed over in the same direction, or patches of unwanted color may appear.

Another trick is to carry extra colors along, hiding them in chains. To do this, however, means that two shuttles or two balls of thread must be manipulated at one time when making the chain, something that is not always practical. When making rings with chains, one color or the other is dropped and picked up again when the next chain is begun.

Shaded (*ombré*) threads or yarns such as can be found in size 70 crochet cotton and 4-ply knitting worsted, or which can be home-dyed, can be used if the design is free enough to encompass the accidental placement of the colors, but the modern worker will probably prefer to blend colors in the total piece by varying them from row to row or working different sections in different colors. Plan these different sections carefully before starting to work, because continuous threads are necessary to avoid unsightly joins. The joins can be hidden, in some cases, by the judicious use of a bead or other found object. Color effects achieved by varying rows and small sections are generally more lively and interesting than those created with a single color. If a piece of purple work, for instance, is to be viewed from a distance, it can be worked in alternate rows of red and blue, rather than in purple alone.

Figure 5-21. Almost-solid tatting. In this sample, made with yellow nylon mason line, the rings were kept as small as possible, and all joins were made *without* the benefit of picots. (Courtesy of Tom Paddock.)

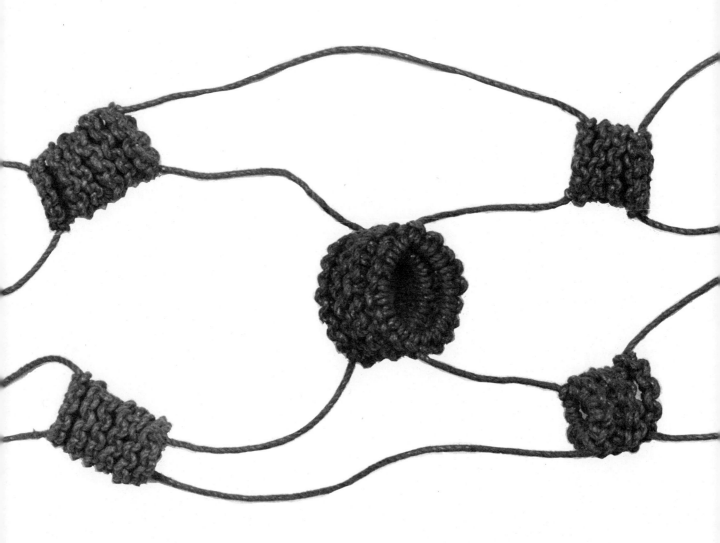

Figure 6-1. The bobble. The author invented a new unit of tatting, which can be varied with ease for many uses. It is described on page 88.

6/Breaking the Rules

Discovering new forms is not difficult if you allow yourself to experiment freely. Once you are familiar with the basic "rule" of tatting, using a single thread to form knots that slide along a knot-bearer, you can open up a whole new world for yourself by manipulating your tools and materials as if you were playing a game. Part of the time at least think of the activity of tatting, not the tatted piece, as an enjoyable end in itself. Don't concern yourself with making something but only with doing something, in just the same way that a game of solitaire is an end in itself.

You will have no finished work to show for your time and effort, but you will have learned a new manner of thinking. The next time you plan a piece, you will find that the tired old procedures are refreshed, as your mind has begun to understand them in a new way. Rolf Hartung's idea of "creative play" with thread and fabric in *Creative Textile Design* served as a springboard for these ideas of unsystematic variation on the techniques of tatting.

The Chinese philosopher Lao Tsu said "a journey of a thousand miles begins under one's foot." Try out immediately any slight variations that occur to you, paying no attention at all to whether or not experiment follows the traditional rules of tatting. The single steps involved in small changes will suggest further changes, and you will be surprised at how the whole will have added up to a considerable "journey." It is not necessary or even desirable to cover large areas in one leap.

The rest of this chapter suggests ways to go and areas to explore. But since the basic goal is to stimulate your own creativity, the examples are offered only as illustrations to get you started. Instead of copying these variations, let them suggest further changes, and let those changes lead you in your own direction. Do not feel discouraged if the going is slow at first.

Variation in rings

In all of tatting, the rings themselves probably offer the least fertile field for basic experimentation, although the differing placement of groups of rings has been the traditional source of variation in tatting patterns, as described in Chapter 5. Nevertheless, the free association of ideas about rings can sometimes bring about happy discoveries.

Must a ring be built up only of double tatting knots? At one time, half stitches were sometimes used (see page 71). The twisting effect of such rings can be exploited to advantage. Picots made in such rings are unstable, and pull out easily. Experimentation with them may lead to something interesting.

To illustrate more clearly how productive small changes can be, and how one gives rise to another, one session concentrating on the ring is described here in detail. Using a shuttle and cotton cable twist, I began a ring, winding the shuttle twice over the ring thread (fig. 6-2). I quickly discovered that the first knot had to be held firmly until the ring was closed, or it would twist around and nullify the effects of the winding. This meant that only small rings could be made that way. Six double knots in a ring was about the largest I could manage at all easily. The rings had a toothed outline somewhat different from ordinary tatting (fig. 6-3a), although it remained to be seen whether or not the difference was great enough to be of any real value.

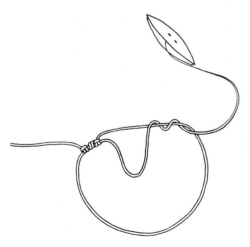

Figure 6-2. Winding the shuttle twice over the ring thread between each knot.

I also noticed that, once the ring was closed, the second winding was never very tight, and would easily accommodate a crochet hook, so that it could be used for joining just as though it were a picot. Once, by accident, I poked the hook through the bar at the top of the double knot, and saw that it was quite loose. With this particular thread, at least, these bars can always be used for joining.

I made several more trials with the crochet cotton, varying the number and placement of both knots and windings. The resulting rings tended to be quite irregular in shape, and it seemed likely that this feature could be exaggerated by using heavier material. Accordingly, I substituted heavy satin cord for the crochet cotton. A ring of three double stitches, each separated by two windings, produced a chunky, roughly triangular shape with virtually no central opening (fig. 6-3b). Four knots, each separated by two windings, produced a square (fig. 6-3c). However, this was the largest ring I could make with any ease at all, although, conceivably, someone with larger hands could do better. These two shapes seemed interesting and might possibly be of use to me at some time in the future. Since no further ideas along these lines presented themselves, I laid aside the satin cord and again picked up the shuttle and heavy crochet cotton.

This time, I worked with the second half of the tatting knot. Before the bearing thread was reversed and the knot pulled tight, I took the same stitch a second time over the ring thread (fig. 6-4) which formed a very pretty little self-padded ring with a beveled edge (fig. 6-3d). Next, I made a similar ring with a picot. When I tried the same idea with the first half of the tatting stitch, the result, though different, was disappointing.

Following the same line of experiment, I formed a ring of double stitches by doubling each half of the knot. This resulted in a solid, chunky ring that looked as though it might contrast well with the ordinary kind. Therefore, I worked a series alternating first one kind of ring and then the other, and joining them together (fig. 6-3e), but, although the new ring took up more space, there was not really enough difference to show.

Another idea presented itself. I began a ring with a double stitch and then picked up with the fingers of the right hand the part of the ring thread over which the next stitch would normally be taken. After twisting this thread five times, I drew the shuttle up through the loop to the right of the twists (fig. 6-5). By alternately pulling on the shuttle thread and stretching out the ring thread, the twists were bunched up and brought close to the last double knot that had been made. The ring

Figure 6-3. Experimental forms of rings. Some are not different enough to make them worthwhile, but each served as a step toward the next invention.

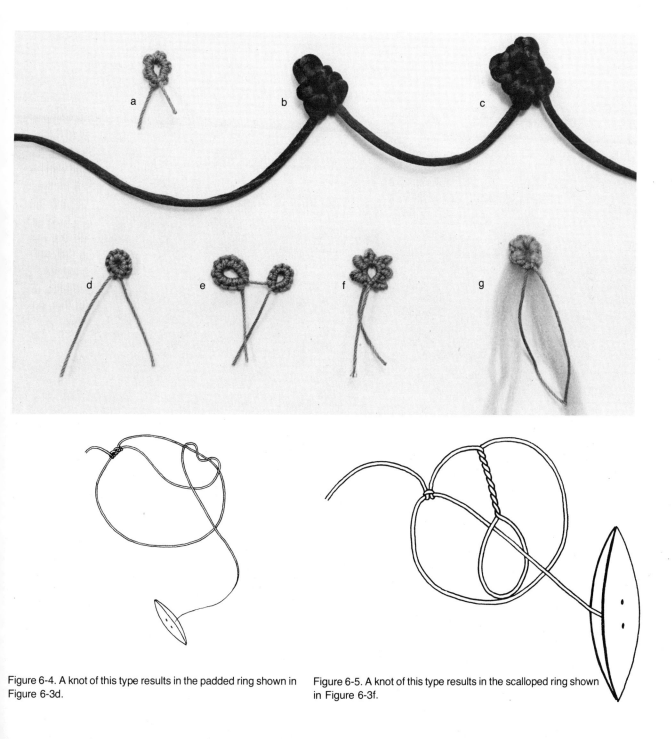

Figure 6-4. A knot of this type results in the padded ring shown in Figure 6-3d.

Figure 6-5. A knot of this type results in the scalloped ring shown in Figure 6-3f.

which resulted from alternating this twisting with double stitches had a deep scalloped edge and an interesting texture (fig. 6-3f). Furthermore, it was obvious that it would be easy to mount beads around a ring using the same technique without the twists (see figs. 7-25 and 7-26). The session wound up with a ring consisting of double stitches alternating with three twists of the ring thread. However, this did not prove very profitable.

If you are very dexterous, see what can be accomplished by working extra threads into the ring. One way of doing this allows you to make rings which consist of knots of alternating colors and textures or both. Using a shuttle wound with heavy crochet cotton, and a ball of fuzzy thread in a contrasting color, polypropylene perhaps, make a ring with the thread wound on the shuttle, but instead of stretching it over all the fingers, bring it back after it has gone around the middle finger. Next make a ring with the thread on the ball, but this ring should bypass the middle finger and go around the fourth and fifth fingers only (fig. 6-6). Picking up the shuttle, make double stitches alternately first on one ring and then on the other. Figure 6-3g shows a ring made in this way.

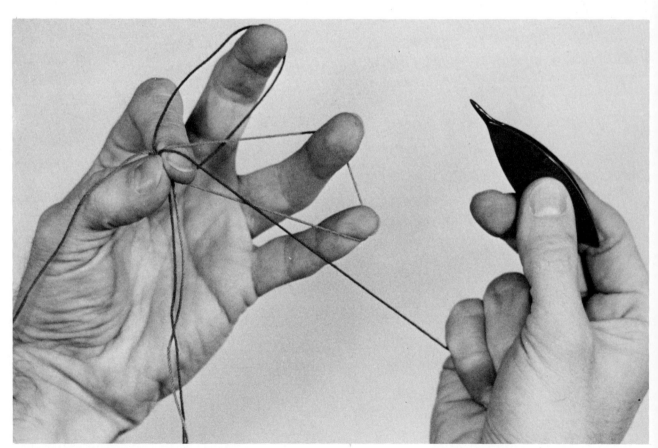

Figure 6-6. Working an extra thread into a ring, such as the ring shown in Figure 6-3g.

Variation in chains

You need only look at Mrs. Pullan's designs (see figs. 1-23 and 3-48) to realize that there is more than one way to make a chain. Being structurally more flexible, chains are easier to experiment with than rings. However, it is possible to go around in circles with chains, too, spending much effort to get only the same result. For instance, reversing the work and making chains between rings in the usual way requires only one shuttle. Exactly the same chains can be made without reversing the work and without changing the knot-bearer, but it takes two shuttles to do it.

Rings cannot be closed unless the bearing thread is reversed properly each time a knot is made. But why must the rule necessarily be followed when making chains? The zigzag formation in Figure 6-7 was the result of this kind of thinking. It was made with a shuttle and a ball of heavy thread, using two colors. The chain began with five double stitches, but continued with five stitches in which the bearing thread was not reversed. This alternation produced a change in color as well as direction.

Since two threads or cords, one of which is carried along inside as the knot-bearer, are needed to make chains, it is possible to create padded chains by using something very heavy for the bearing thread in all or part of the work. The heavy-weight soft cord used for piping, or parcel-post twine, can be tried. However, it is usually desirable to choose some-thing that approximates the ball thread in color, since there are chinks in the covering knots through which a contrasting hue can show, detracting from the work. Those who like to get out the dyepot at the least excuse might investigate whether the soft dressmaker's cords take dye easily.

Incidentally, rings can also be padded if desired by introducing an extra thread. Since the thick thread must not show, form the ring thread around the fingers, only with the tatting thread, which is wound on the shuttle. Then, grasping the end of the padding between the thumb and forefinger of the left hand, lay its length along the shuttle thread and manipulate the two threads as though they were one.

When rag rugs were popular, a tatter in California made chains using rag strips as though they were wound on a shuttle. For the ball of thread she used heavy cord. Later she coiled the chain around itself and whipped it together with the same heavy cord, although she could also have made picots and attached the work as she went. That might have produced a somewhat more open effect, though, depending on how small a picot she could make with that particular cord. Attaching a new rag strip when the old one is about to run out would be a simple matter of sewing the ends together with a few firm stitches, thus eliminating the extra bulk that a knot or much overlapping would produce.

Figure 6-7. Experimental chain, in which the bearing thread is not reversed in alternating sections.

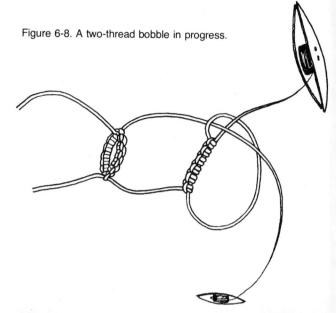

Figure 6-8. A two-thread bobble in progress.

Three-dimensional forms

Must all tatting be flat? Such sculptural forms as the traditional tatted basket stiffened with starch or the old-fashioned tassel top, a bell-shaped ornamental cover for the top part of a tassel, which was often tatted, are proof that three-dimensional forms are possible. Contemporary textile craftsmen are scrutinizing all thread techniques to see how they can adapt them to sculptural forms, and tatting brings some unique qualities to this area.

In addition to the fact that tatting can easily be made into a tube by joining the end of the last ring or chain to the beginning of the first, there is a possibility of overlapping, twisting, or bending the various elements of tatting to give a new look while still keeping the work essentially flat. This idea does not seem to have been explored at all by tatters.

As you have already seen, a chain made up only of one half of the tatting knot has a built-in twist. Such forms are used to good advantage in macramé. Why not in tatting? Picots do not always have to be kept flat; long ones can be made that are intended to be bent across the ring and held there by joining in some fashion, or they can be woven through the rings. Long rings can be made and twisted or bent in some way. Various areas of the work can be overlapped. All joining does not have to be done by means of picots; there are holes in the centers of rings and structural threads loose enough to pull the joining loop through. One kind of tatting can be worked over another, as, for instance, a background of large, fairly plain rings, embellished with rows of much finer, more elaborate tatting worked over, around, under, or through it.

All of these suggestions and more are possible, but it is up to you to find out whether you will gain any advantage in applying them. There is a fertile field here for imagination and ingenuity.

An especially useful three-dimensional form is the bobble, which I discovered through "creative play." One example is seen in Figure 6-1, and another in the body of the butterfly in color on page 40. To make a two-thread bobble, tat a ring of any size and when it is half made, catch a thread wound on a second shuttle between the ring and shuttle threads before continuing (fig. 6-8). When the ring has been closed, begin another ring with the second shuttle and catch the first thread in that ring. The possibilities are infinite since the rings can be made close together or far apart, as many more threads as desired can be introduced, and many different colors, textures, or weights of thread can be combined.

Figure 6-9. Detail, 2 inches wide, of design for belt, neckpiece, etc. Double overlapping circles are made with several pairs of threads, and reverse is same as front. These rings are made with several pairs of threads in a macramé technique. (Courtesy Joan Michaels Paque. Photograph by Hank Paque.)

Figure 6-10. Nylon neckpiece in tatting and wrapping, 10½ x 12 inches. This shows the typical way to combine tatting with multiple-thread techniques such as macramé and bobbin lace. (Courtesy of Joan Michaels Paque. Photograph by Hank Paque.)

Tatting combinations

Tatting as a multiple-element textile. Although tatting, along with knitting, crocheting, and needlepoint lace, is classed as a single-element textile, the introduction of work with a second shuttle took it a step down the road toward becoming a multiple-element process. As tatting is used in macramé, work with groups of threads comes into the picture, as can be seen in Figures 6-9 and 6-10. Further thinking along these lines produced fabric like that shown in Figure 6-11, where rings of various colors are joined together and the chains interlaced.

Tatting and other thread work. One feature of contemporary work in handmade textiles is the mixture of various thread techniques. In the nineteenth and early twentieth centuries, tatting was often combined with crochet, needlepoint lace, hairpin lace, embroidery, and needleweaving. Because it is so difficult to make a really solid area using tatting alone, experimentation along these lines is especially useful.

Figure 6-11. Rings of various colors of acrylic rug yarn are joined together with the chains interlaced.

Weavers may find it interesting to invent ways to add tatting to their work. A series of tatted rings, separated by lengths of thread can be incorporated as part of the weft so that the rings hang free (fig. 6-14). Knotted lines can also be incorporated as part of the weft, as shown in color on page 37. When working on a loom, it is useful to know that rings may also be made sailor-fashion by tying knots over a ring thread without changing the knot bearer (fig. 6-15). This method cannot be used to make a series of closely spaced rings, however.

Of great potential value when weaving small tapestries, or to anyone who works with stitchery, is the ability to form tatting on the same thread with only a needle. Here is how it is done: Thread a needle and twist the separate parts of the double knot onto it as shown in Figures 6-16 and 6-17. When the desired number of knots has been made in this way, pull the thread through. The thread is then free to continue with further tatting formations or to return to making the weft or the form of stitchery in progress.

Tatting and other objects. Tatting can be decorated in many ways, primarily with beads (see Chapter 7). But linear material such as braid can be alternated with rows of tatting or, as previously mentioned, large plaques of metal, ceramic, wood, or other material can be included to form solid areas in the design. Found objects can be worked in or tied to a fringe.

Tatting can be used inside other materials, as long as an appropriate way of attaching the threads is devised. Although the rings pictured in Figure 6-19 were ultimately hung as a mobile, that was an afterthought, and the individual pieces were actually fashioned by free experimentation. The base of each ring is a hoop with ends cut at an angle. Number 4 reed (not necessarily the best material for this purpose) was soaked until pliable, after which the ends were glued together. It is possible to work from the outside in, or, if a symmetrical center is wanted, to make a circular piece and then suspend it within the hoop. Cover the hoop with tatting, all at once or as the warp progresses, then attach the center by crocheting or sewing with a tapestry needle. If you want to tat only the center without tatting over the hoop, try buttonhole stitch as used in needlepoint lace (see fig. 4-1). This provides an attractive covering for the hoop although the stitches have a tendency to twist.

Figure 6-12. Doily with tatted wheels, nineteenth century. The design closely resembles the tatted Irish pattern shown earlier in Figure 1-13, but the centers are crocheted. (Courtesy of Oregon Historical Society.)

Figure 6-13. Detail of insertion, early nineteenth century, ⅝ inch wide. The chain on either side appears to be crocheted, and is attached through the picots on the rings, just as a tatted chain might be. (Courtesy of The Costume and Textile Study Collection, School of Home Economics, University of Washington. Photograph by William Eng.)

Figure 6-14. Something for weavers — tatted rings, separated by lengths of thread, can be incorporated as weft in such a way that the rings hang free.

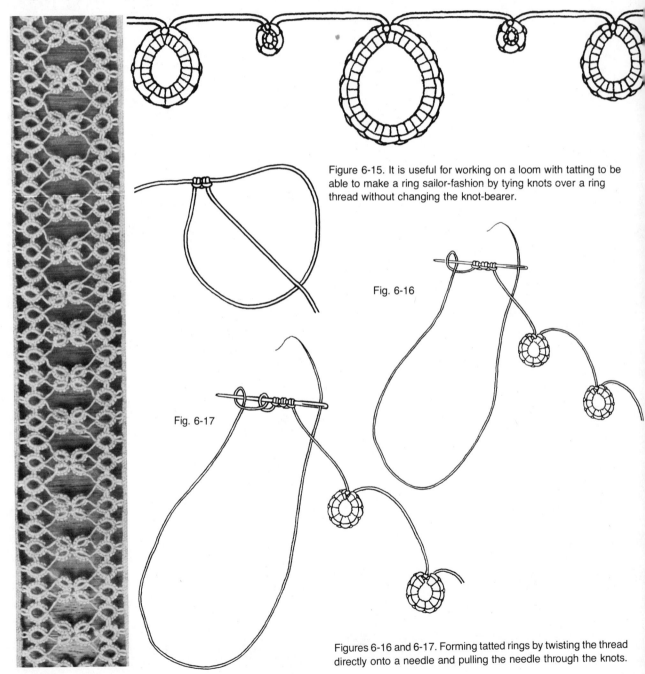

Figure 6-15. It is useful for working on a loom with tatting to be able to make a ring sailor-fashion by tying knots over a ring thread without changing the knot-bearer.

Fig. 6-16

Fig. 6-17

Figures 6-16 and 6-17. Forming tatted rings by twisting the thread directly onto a needle and pulling the needle through the knots.

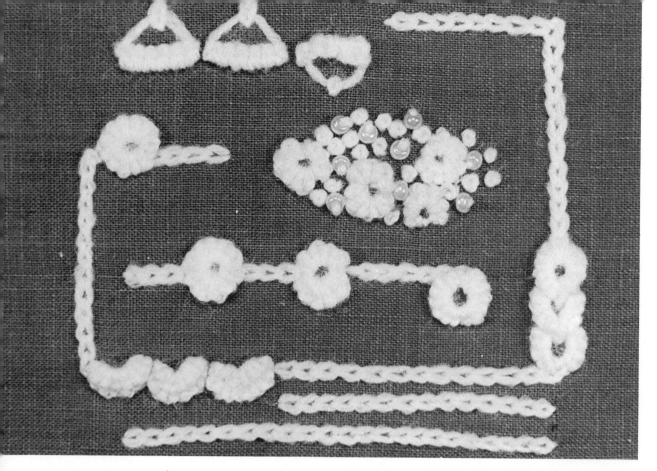

Figure 6-18. Embroidered sampler, white acrylic sport yarn on linen, incorporating tatted rings made directly on the needle. The oval is textured with tatted rings, French knots, and small beads. Immediately below, a row of tatted rings alternates with chain stitch. At top left, the rings have not been closed. The needle is taken back down into the fabric at the end of the row of knots and the bearing thread caught down with a detached chain stitch. At the lower right, the rings are overlapped by beginning each ring in the center of the last. At lower left, the rings are folded over themselves and tacked. The tatted rings can also be left standing at right angles to the fabric.

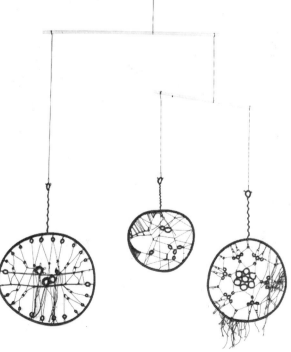

Figure 6-19. Experiment with hoops, using cotton cable twist and pearl cotton. (Courtesy of Tom Paddock.)

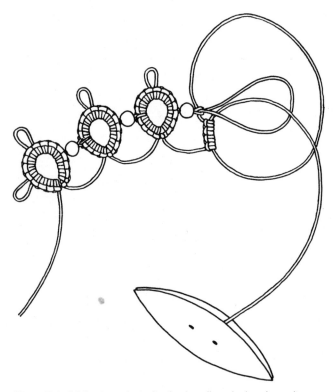

Figure 7-1. Joining to a picot after having slipped a bead over it.

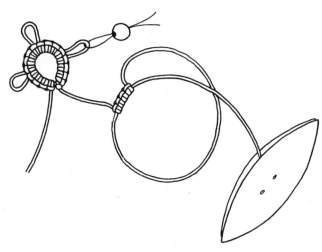

Figure 7-2. Easing a small-holed bead over a picot with the aid of a short length of sewing thread.

Figure 7-3. Girdle (belt) of white rayon satin cord with ceramic beads. This design is essentially a continuous chain which is connected to itself at intervals by means of picots. Beads are slipped over the picots before joining.

7/Adding Sparkle

Beaded Fabric and Jewelry

The idea of adding beads or sequins to tatting is by no means new. The traditional way of doing it, discussed below, was to string the beads on the ball thread and slip them into place as the work progressed. There are much easier ways to mount beads, based on using the picots or joining to a cord strung with beads. In contemporary tatting designs, any object with a hole can be included by using the hole as if it were a picot and joining through it.

Although specific instructions are included for some of the objects pictured in this chapter, the primary purpose is to illustrate in detail the methods under discussion. If you try to work any of these patterns, remember that, even though you use the same threads shown in the models, you may have to adjust the number of knots given, unless beads of identical size are chosen.

Mounting beads by using picots

This method, far easier and more useful than the traditional one, consists in slipping a bead over a picot before joining another part of the work to that picot (fig. 7-1). Care must be taken while forming the ring to make the picot long enough to hold the bead and *also* allow for the connection. If the hole in the bead is large enough so that it can be slipped over a crochet hook, the picot may be drawn through the bead and the thread brought up for joining in one motion. Otherwise it will be found best to slip a short length of sewing cotton through the picot and then thread the bead onto the picot by means of the doubled cotton (fig. 7-2). Leave the cotton in place until the join is completed. Many beads that could be added to a picot only with difficulty or not at all, present no problem when this trick is used.

Beaded girdle (belt). The girdle in Figure 7-3 combines this way of adding beads ("crow" beads of about 6mm are used) with a design that consists entirely of chains. Remember that all picots must be long enough to hold a bead and also allow for joining.

Use continuous length of rayon satin cord, long enough to complete the girdle. Twenty yards makes about one yard of pattern. Girdle should be made five or six inches longer than waist measurement so that, when fastened, a short length hangs down vertically. Beginning at ends, wind cord into two balls of equal size and secure with rubber bands. Do not cut balls apart. Ch, lds, p, lds. *Rw, change shuttles, ch, 5ds, p, lds. Slip bead over next to last p and join bearing thread to that p. (In this pattern, the bearing thread changes whenever the work is reversed. That should cause no trouble if it is remembered that it is a smooth join with no crossing that is wanted. The thread to be connected is, therefore, the one nearest the picot.) Repeat from * for desired length. To finish, sew large bead or button to beginning of belt, choosing one that harmonizes and is big or small enough to catch securely when fitted into the open spaces of the belt. At the other end, secure last knot by tacking invisibly with needle and thread. Leave ends long and dangling, but knot each once at tip to prevent fraying.

Beaded choker necklace.   A bead may be placed in the center of a four-ring unit by using a variation of this method. The choker in Figure 7-4 is worked along its length, first down one side to make a row of half-clusters, and then returning along the other side with half clusters to complete the quatrefoil forms. The beads (about 4mm) are added on the return journey. Length of thread needed depends on neck size, and a sample should be worked for a closer estimate. The tiny picots should be just large enough to allow a crochet hook to be inserted and a loop drawn through for joining. Attaching the rings to each other around the beads in this way makes for a firmer, more stable piece, but the purpose is defeated if the picots are too large. One or two trials may be needed before the proper length is found for the long picots. They

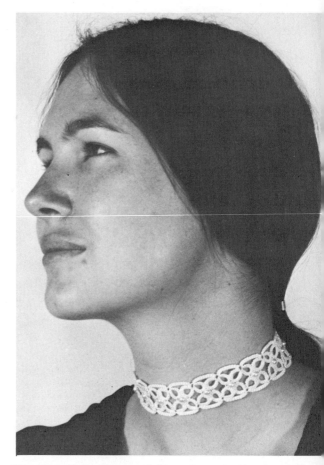

Figure 7-4. Choker of nylon stitching twine worked into four-ring clusters, with small imitation pearls located in the centers of the clusters.

generally have to be somewhat longer than appears necessary at first. The ends of the choker may be left as is for typing, or they may be worked into a clasp of some sort.

Use nylon stitching twine on shuttle and a ball of same thread. *First row:* *R, 5ds, tiny p, 2ds, very long p, 2ds, tiny p, 5ds, cl. Rw, ch, 10ds. Rw, r, 5ds, join to last p of previous r, 2ds, join to very long p of previous r, 2ds, tiny p, 5ds, cl. Repeat from * for desired length. Cut thread, leaving long ends for tying or finishing. *Return journey:* *R, 5ds, join to last p of last r in first row, 2ds, mount bead on last long p of first row and join to that p, 2ds, tiny p, 5ds, cl. Rw, ch, 10ds. Rw, r, 5ds, join to last p of last r made, 2ds, join again to long p where bead was mounted, 2ds, join to adjacent p of previous row, 5ds, cl. Repeat from * to end of row, joining and adding beads in same way to each successive pair of rings in first row.

Tatted purse panel. By using still another variation of this basic method, beads often can be positioned in the centers of rings. The shoulder-strap purse shown in color on page 41 has a tatted panel that is essentially the same design as that used for the choker just described, except that the strip now repeats itself, and rows of small rings with beads in their centers have been added. To make these, work a ring which has a picot at the top. After the ring has been closed, double the shuttle thread for a short distance, and slip a bead down over it (fig. 7-5). The loop that then protrudes from the bead is adjusted in length until it is the same height from the base of the ring as the picot, and the two are tied together temporarily with a short length of thread (fig. 7-6). The design must be planned so that, eventually, another part of the tatting will be joined to this picot and loop as though they were one, thus securing the bead permanently, and the temporary tie can then be pulled out. This temporary tying is time consuming and tedious, but necessary for beginners. Once you have the idea and the knack, the thread can be left the correct length from the start and the bead added when ready to attach a ring or chain permanently to the two loops. Be sure that all of the loops holding beads appear on the same side of the work, unless there is some special reason to do otherwise. Complete directions for the tatted section of the purse follow. The ceramic beads, called "pony" beads, are about 3mm, and

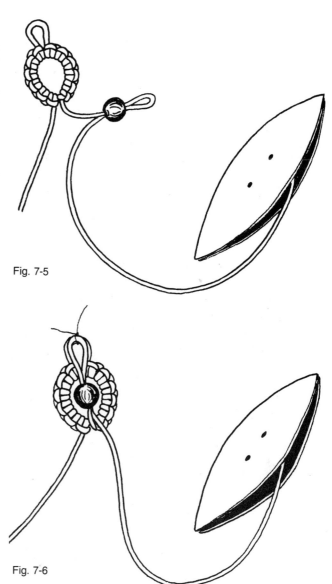

Fig. 7-5

Fig. 7-6

Figures 7-5 and 7-6. Positioning a bead in the center of a ring. The bead is secured permanently by attaching another ring or chain to the two loops that have been tied together.

length of thread depends on size of panel. This design can be varied and adapted for many other objects, such as the wall hanging in Figure 4-10.

Begin with a shuttle wound with cotton cable twist and a ball of the same thread. *First row:* *R, 8ds, tiny p, 2ds, very long p, 2ds, tiny p, 8ds, cl. Rw, ch, 6ds, p, 6ds. Rw, r, 8ds, join to last p of previous r, 2ds, join to very long p of previous r, 2ds, tiny p, 8ds, cl. Repeat from * for desired length. Cut thread, leaving long ends for finishing. *Return journey:* Using two shuttles, *r, 8ds, join to last p of last r in first row, 2ds, mount bead on last long p of first row and join to that p, 2ds, tiny p, 8ds, cl. Rw, ch, 6ds. Change shuttles, r, 6ds, p, 6ds, cl. Draw up loop on shuttle thread, mount bead and secure loop with temporary tie to last p made. Change shuttles, ch, 6ds. Rw, r, 8ds, join to last p of next to last r, 2ds, join again to long p where bead was mounted, 2ds, join to adjacent p of first row, 8ds, cl. Repeat from * to end of row, joining and adding beads to each successive pair of rings in first row. Repeat first row and return journey as often as desired. *Final return journey:* With shuttle and ball of thread, *r, 8ds, join to last p of last r in previous row, 2ds, mount bead on last long p of previous row and join to that p, 2ds, tiny p, 8ds, cl. Rw, ch, 6ds, p, 6ds. Rw, r, 8ds, join to last p of last r made, 2ds, join again to long p where bead was mounted, 2ds, join to adjacent p of previous row, 8ds, cl. Repeat from * to end of row, joining and adding beads to each successive pair of rings in previous row.

Necklace pendant. The necklace in Figure 7-7 combines two of the techniques described above. It consists of five vertical strips of tatting, each worked from the bottom up and in two journeys to complete a motif. A wire choker ring, available in craft and hobby shops is threaded through top picots after piece is completed. As all rows are short, estimating thread length is not necessary. Just wind shuttle, and it won't run out before end of row. The oat-shaped beads are 6½mm, round beads are 5mm.

Use a shuttle wound with nylon stitching twine and same thread on a ball. *R, 10ds, p (long enough to hold round bead), 10ds, cl. Sp (twice distance from bottom to top of ring just made, not counting picot). Ch, 5ds, 6p sep by 2ds, 3ds (fig. 7-8). Form loop where space was left and put long bead over loop (figs. 7-8 and 7-9). Turn r so that it lies over bead, and put loop that holds bead over p at top of r (fig. 7-10). Slip round bead over this p, then join end of ch to p, thus securing both beads (fig. 7-11). Repeat from *. (Notice that, in making the second and all succeeding repeats, the space left after completing the ring that will hold the bead occurs only on the shuttle thread. The first knot in the chain of the second half-ring is made up close to the last knot in the chain of the first half-ring.) *Return journey* (fig. 7-12): Having joined to p of last r, continue ch without cutting threads. *Ch, 3ds, 6p sep by 2ds, 5ds, join to base of r. Repeat from * till end of strip is reached. Finish by making an overhand knot at base of last r, thus uniting all four loose threads. To make necklace, form strip of eight units, two strips of seven units, and two strips of six units. As work progresses, join as shown. It is the two center picots of each chain that are joined. Work units where single, long bead occurs as follows: Sp (twice length of bead to be mounted), ch 5ds, 6p sep by 2ds, 3ds. Form loop where space was left and put bead over loop. Join ch to top of loop to secure bead.

Figure 7-7. Necklace pendant of nylon stitching twine. The basic design unit includes two beads of different shapes which are mounted piggyback one above the other.

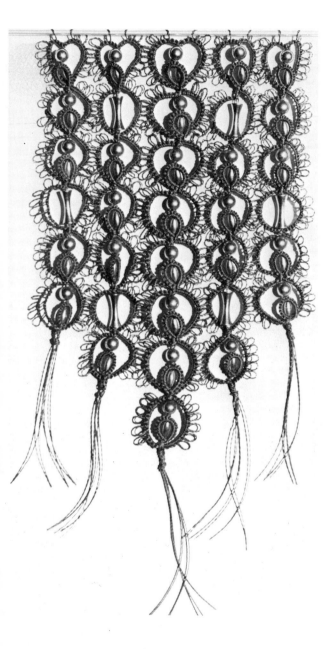

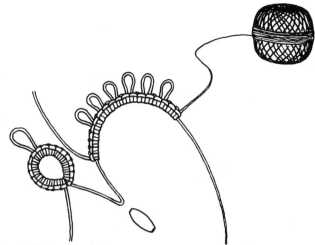

Figure 7-8. Mounting the beads for the necklace pendant. Having completed a ring with a picot at the top large enough to hold a *round* bead, leave a length of thread, which, when doubled, is long enough to hold a *long* bead. Then make the chain.

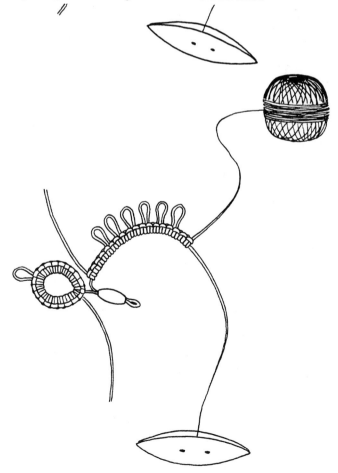

Figure 7-9. Next, double the length of thread and slip the bead over it.

Figure 7-10. Then turn the ring so that it lies over the bead, and, with a crochet hook, put the loop that holds the bead over the picot at the top of the ring.

Figure 7-11. Finally, slip the round bead over the picot and join the chain to it in the usual way.

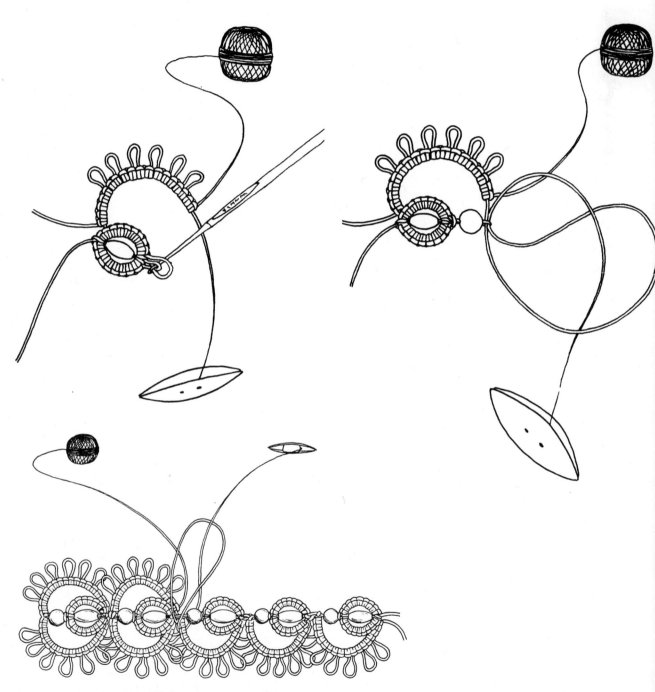

Figure 7-12. Complete the motifs by a return row, as shown.

The traditional way to add beads

In the past, when tatting was to be beaded, the beads were usually strung on the tatting cotton and pushed down into the work as required. Generally, it was the chains that were embellished in this way (fig. 7-13), since it is easier to put beads on the ball thread than to manipulate a shuttle filled with what is essentially a string of beads.

Nevertheless, we do sometimes want to string beads on the shuttle thread in order to mount them on rings or along the inner edges of chains. This is somewhat more difficult, but possible, although, obviously, not always feasible. When threading beads on the shuttle thread, there are a couple of points to watch. First, in preparing the shuttle, care must be taken to distribute the beads fairly evenly so that neither too many nor too few are on hand at any one time. A little practice will show how to manage this. Second, in making rings, if beads are to be positioned at picots or are to go between knots on the outer side of the ring, all beads needed for a particular ring must be placed on the ring thread *before* the first knot is tied (figs. 7-14 and 7-15). Those that remain on the shuttle thread (fig. 7-16) can only be strung thereafter on the bearing thread, and they will then appear on the inside of the ring.

Beaded hanging.   The beads in the rami hanging, shown in color on page 41, were pre-strung. Each vertical row was worked from bottom to top with a single, continuous thread. A jumbo yarn bobbin was used, and, by being careful not to pile beads on top of one another, but rather laying them side by side, half on either side of the bobbin, the shuttle was kept manageable. However, adding more beads to make a longer hanging with a continuous thread would have been impractical. In tatting of this kind, the amount of thread needed for each row is calculated by working a two-ring sample with a premeasured length of thread, subtracting the amount not used, and multiplying the rest, which was used, by the number of rings to be made. Allow a generous extra length as a margin for error. Unfortunately, the rami, even though it was used double, proved a little too soft, and the hanging has to be refurbished whenever it is subjected to any amount of handling. Thread with more body (nylon stitching twine, perhaps) would have served better. In spite of this shortcoming, the technique used for the design is interesting and useful, and complete instructions follow. When working, the beads remain on the shuttle thread until placed.

First row: String eleven beads and wind on shuttle. *R, 12ds, 3p sep by 12ds, 12ds, cl. Push a bead down close to base of r, then, bringing shuttle thread up behind r, join to center p (fig. 7-17). Repeat from * until all beads have been used. Make twelfth r. Unwind thread from bobbin, string, and secure another bead. *Second row:* String 3 beads. Work three rings with beads, joining first p of each to third p of corresponding r in first row. Sp, r, 7ds, join to last p of fourth r of first row, 7ds, cl. Sp, r, 7ds, p, 7ds, cl. Continue to top of row, joining alternate rings to first row and ending with one that contains a bead by unwinding and stringing bead as in first row. All other rows are constructed in the same way. Arrange and join them as in the photograph of the piece.

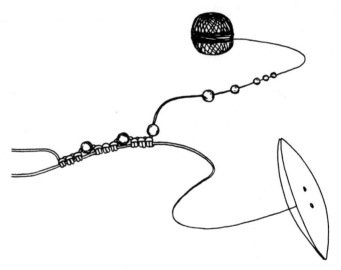

Figure 7-13. The traditional way to add beads is to string them on the ball thread and then push them into place as necessary.

Figures 7-14, 7-15, and 7-16. If you are very dextrous, and want
to thread beads on the shuttle thread, remember that what will
appear on the outer side of the ring must be placed on the ring
thread before the first knot it tied.

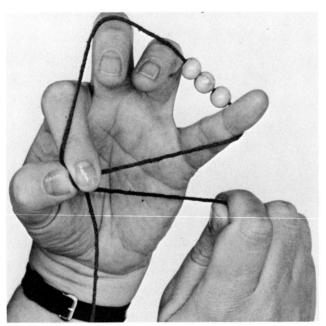

Fig. 7-14

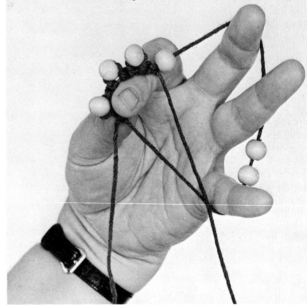

Fig. 7-15

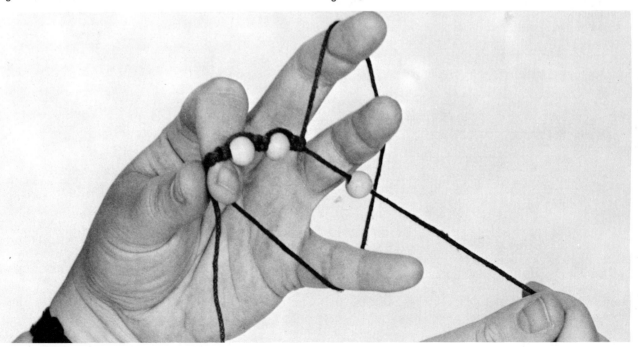

Fig. 7-16

Figure 7-17. Mounting prestrung beads in the centers of rings, as in the beaded hanging.

Tatted motifs around large beads

Here is an easy and secure way to work a design around a large central bead. The bead chosen must have a hole large enough to accomodate a doubled thread. The directions are for the pendant and necklace shown in color on page 44, but single shells, beads, or other found objects with holes through them could be used in many designs. The pearls were 4mm, and the colored pony beads 3mm. Estimating the length of thin thread used here is not important because a shuttle full will not run out in the middle of a piece.

Bead pendant and necklace

Center bead

Wind shuttle with nylon stitching twine, but do not cut thread. Instead, start a ch, leaving loop at beginning which is a bit longer than diameter of bead (fig. 7-18). When ch, which should have several picots in it, is long enough to reach halfway around bead from one end of hole to the other, thread doubled loop through bead and join work to end of loop which now protrudes from bead (fig. 7-19). Continue ch around bead, and when beginning is reached, join again so that ch encircles bead (fig. 7-20). Knot securely and cut thread.

Directions follow for the pendant and necklace. When making a circular design of this kind, there should not be too much play in any of the picots that hold beads or the result will be floppy and unattractive.

Pendant

Circle center bead as explained above with ch, leave loop, 2ds, 5p sep by 2ds (picots must be large enough to hold two small beads), lds. Thread loop at beginning of ch through hole in large bead and join. Continue ch: lds, 5p sep by 2ds, 2ds, join, thus completing circle. Knot thread securely. Cut both threads, leaving long ends. For rest of pendant, use shuttle and ball of thread. *Second round:* *R, 4ds, mount two beads on p immediately to right of cut ends in ch that circles central bead, join to that p, 4ds, cl. Rw, ch, 2ds, 3p sep by 2ds (picots are to hold single beads), 2ds. Rw. Repeat from * until ten rings and ten chains have been made. R, 4ds, small p, 4ds, cl. Rw, ch, 2ds, 3p sep by 2ds, 2ds. Without twisting, tie to base of first r and cut threads.

Figures 7-18, 7-19, and 7-20. Circling a large bead with tatting. Begin a chain, leaving a loop at the beginning which is a bit longer than the diameter of the bead. When the chain, which should have several picots in it so that more tatting may be added, is

long enough to reach halfway around the bead, thread the doubled loop through the bead and join the chain to the loop. Then continue the chain around the bead, and join again so that chain encircles the bead, tie firmly, and cut.

Thread two beads onto cut ends of ch that circle bead, put one of these ends through p in last r made in second round, and tie securely. *Third round:* R, 2ds, slip bead over center p of any ch in previous round, join to that p, 2ds, cl. *Rw, ch, 4ds, p, 4ds. Rw, r, 2ds, slip bead over next p in previous round and join to that p, 2ds, add bead to next p, join, 2ds, cl. Rw, ch, 4ds, p, 4ds. Rw, r, 2ds, slip bead over next p, 2ds, cl. Repeat from * around. Tie and cut.

Necklace

To avoid knots at points where necklace is attached to pendant, calculate amount of thread needed for half of necklace and cut this off with a generous allowance for error. Beginning at ends, wind measured thread onto two shuttles, half on one and half on the other. Do not cut shuttles apart. **With either shuttle, r, 5ds, join to any p in outer row of pendant, 5ds, cl. *R, 5ds, p (long enough to hold a bead), 5ds, cl. Rw, ch, 5ds, p, 5ds. Rw, r, 5ds, mount bead on p of last r, and join to that p, 5ds, cl. Rw, change shuttles.‡ Repeat from * until half the necklace is made, but end with a ch. Rewind shuttles and repeat from **, this time joining to p in outer row of pendant adjacent to one joined to first time. Be sure this end of necklace is facing right way. It should be mirror image of other half. When necklace is of desired length, end at ‡. R, 5ds, mount bead on p of last r in first half of necklace, join to that p, 5ds, cl. Be sure, before doing so, that necklace is not twisted, and that both final rings are on same side of ch. If not, make one more unit. Tie and cut.

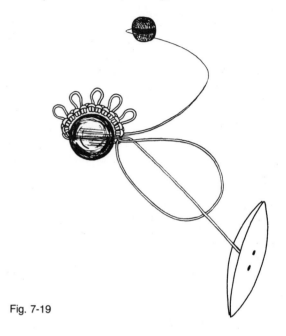

Fig. 7-19

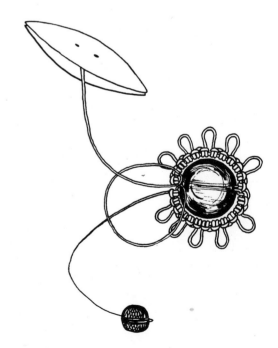

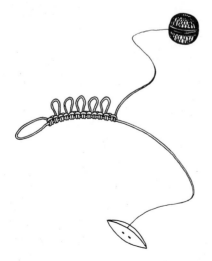

Fig, 7-18

Fig. 7-20

Other ways to mount beads

It is also possible to string beads relatively loosely on a separate thread and to join tatting to that thread from one or both sides (fig. 7-21). The bead-strung cord must be carefully secured at both ends upon completion of the work. A string of oval beads handled this way and caught alternately first from one side and then the other results in a zigzag line that resembles one kind of old-fashioned braid (fig. 7-22).

Sequins and cluster beads, or any other flat object with a hole or holes, may be joined to just as though joining to a picot. Figure 7-24 shows how this is done. The technique makes it possible to incorporate pieces of metal, ceramic, or heavy leather into wall hangings and other objects. In fact, anything that can have holes punched or drilled into it may be handled this way.

For the necklace shown in color on page 44, chains were worked around the beads, entering the hole three times (see fig. 7-24), thus forming units which could be joined at the picots as the work progressed. Upon completion of each unit, the ends were tied, cut, and, since nylon stitching twine was used, glued. White glue is satisfactory. Beware of nail polish and other materials with similar solvents when using plastic beads. For the pendant, six units were formed into a circle around which further tatting was worked, after which the needlepoint center was added.

Interesting effects can sometimes be achieved if large beads, particularly those that are unusual in shape, and, perhaps graduated in size, are mounted on heavy thread in the following way: Having made one or more double knots in a ring, pull the ring thread, where the next stitches would normally be made, into a loop and slip a bead over the loop (fig. 7-25). Secure the bead by putting the shuttle through the loop and drawing the threads up tight. In doing so, be careful to see that the bead is positioned correctly so that the ring thread is not pushed out of line and so that the bead has a frame of thread around it. Since no knot or twist has been made in the bearing thread, the ring can be closed in the usual way. Figure 7-26 shows how the finished ring should look, and, of course, as many beads as desired may be mounted on one ring. This same method can be used to add beads to chains.

It is, of course, possible to complete the tatting and then add beads by sewing them on. However, beads or sequins actually incorporated into the work are usually much more satisfactory, and, with so many possible ways to do it, sewing them on afterward is a technique that should be reserved for objects that get little wear, like wall hangings, and for times when a finished piece that is a bit drab or just seems to miss the mark can be retrieved by adding a decorative piece or two.

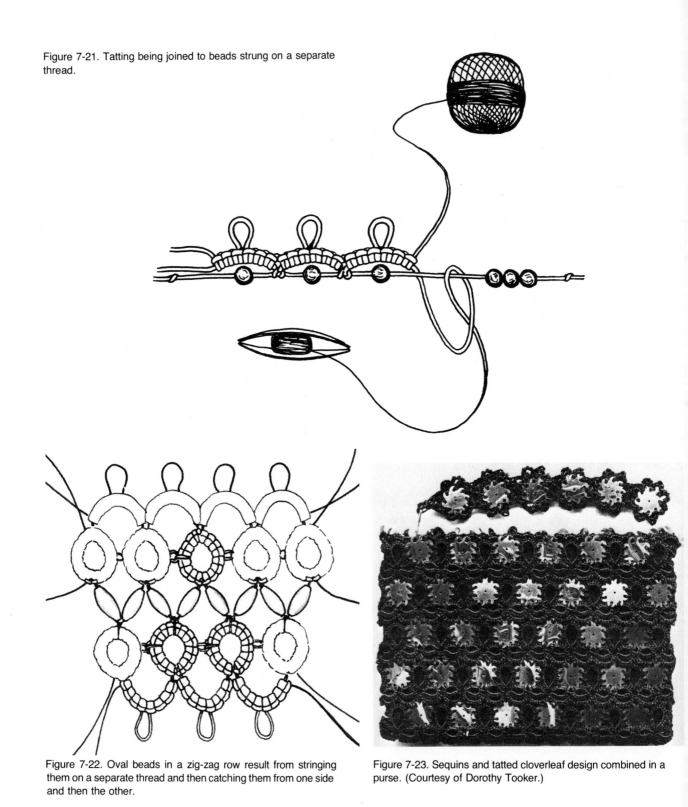

Figure 7-21. Tatting being joined to beads strung on a separate thread.

Figure 7-22. Oval beads in a zig-zag row result from stringing them on a separate thread and then catching them from one side and then the other.

Figure 7-23. Sequins and tatted cloverleaf design combined in a purse. (Courtesy of Dorothy Tooker.)

Figure 7-24. Joining to a flat object with a hole in it, in this case a cluster bead. The ring thread is brought up through the hole as though the hole were a picot.

Fig. 7-25

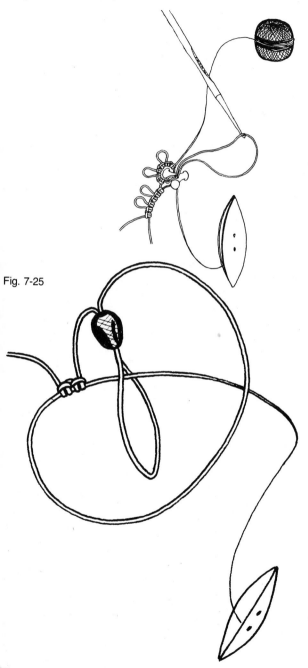

Figure 7-27. Evening mitts. The small, round sequins at the cuffs are carried on the picots of chains. They were prestrung on the tatting thread. (Courtesy of Dorothy Tooker.)

Figures 7-25 and 7-26. Mounting a bead on the ring thread, so that it is framed by a loop of thread. As many beads as desired can be mounted on a ring this way.

Fig. 7-26

Figure 7-28. Necklace of heavy polypropylene macramé cord.

Tatted jewelry

Jewelry made with cotton thread or rami will begin to look worn in far too short a time to warrant the amount of work that must go into it. Materials that withstand friction far better are nylon and linen. It is obvious that scratchy materials should be avoided if the piece is to be worn next to the skin, but are suitable for brooches and pins. Satisfactory metallic threads are difficult to find, and, of those, many can only be used for chains.

Nylon stitching twine is about the right weight for all-round use and comes in a range of colors. Be careful, when using it, to secure all ends with glue after tying and before cutting away the excess thread to prevent the knots from opening after a few hours. Once the ends have been cut, they may be too short to retie. If beads are used, check beforehand that the glue you are using will not damage them.

When designing beaded jewelry, the beads should dominate. Either by their quantity or their appearance they should be dominant enough so that the tatting appears to be a setting for them. When designing nonbeaded jewelry, the tatting material is most important.

Tatted collar necklace. Not much more than a simple tatted edging carried out in very heavy thread, this necklace (fig. 7-28) would also be effective worked in satin cord. Many other tatted edgings can be adapted in the same way. The necklace uses about fifty feet of cord.

First make a ring without winding cord on any shuttle: Leaving a six-inch length of cord at beginning of work, r, 10ds, p, 10ds, cl. Cut thread six inches from base of r, so that there are two six-inch strings hanging from ring. Knot each end once near tip to prevent raveling and set r aside. Roll rest of cord into two balls, beginning at ends, and secure with rubber bands. Do not cut balls apart. With either ball, *r, 5ds, p, 5ds, cl. Rw, ch, 20ds. Rw, r, 5ds, join to p of last r, 5ds, cl.** Repeat once from *. R, 5ds, p, 5ds, cl. Rw, ch, 10ds. Change shuttles, r, 5ds, join to p of r that was made first and set aside, 5ds, cl. Change shuttles, ch, 10ds. Rw, r, 5ds, join to p of next-to-last r made, 5ds, cl. Repeat twice from * to **. Cut ends, leaving at least ten inches. Thread one end through base of corresponding r at opposite side of necklace. Knot each end.

Figure 7-29. Ocean-polished black beach pebbles and fine white tatting are combined to form earrings. (Courtesy Lynda Ford Voris. In the author's collection.)

Figure 7-30. Earrings made with colored tatting cotton and assorted beads. (Courtesy of Lynda Ford Voris. In the author's collection.)

Tatted earrings have long been a favorite, and the simplest ones are small motifs glued to earring backs. These can be made with or without beads. Any of the pattern units in Chapter 5 could be adapted easily to earrings.

A kind of plique à jour effect is achieved by immersing tatted motifs in dipping plastic. If fine thread is used, the first bath must be a dilute solution or, instead of being filled with plastic, the picots will close up.

Like knitting and crochet, tatting can be simply a vehicle for mounting beads. In the earrings in Figure 7-31, the tatting is almost completely hidden by the beads. For this effect, use thread that is relatively fine in relation to the beads. String the beads on the ball thread and tat chains, placing a bead between each knot. The earrings shown are of tatting cotton and seed beads, but it would be worthwhile to try the technique using less conventional materials. The chains may be arranged and joined in any way desired.

Figure 7-31. Earrings using tatting as a device for holding seed beads together. (Courtesy of Susan E. Munstedt. In the author's collection.)

Figure 8-1. Tatted panel. The flowers were made first from DMC 6-cord, size 70 cotton, and laid on a sheet of paper. A cartoon was then drawn for the figure of the girl. The mesh ground was worked last and is a single, continuous thread of size 150 cotton. The bodice is crocheted.

Handwork in a Machine Age

While a person who has never made anything for his own use with his own hands ought certainly to have the experience, it is also true that too many of us are concerned with making things for use when we ought not to be. The machine has carried part of the world a long way from the time when, given the difficulty of producing all the raw and manufactured products that were necessary to fill basic needs, it was foolish to squander any scrap of material. Yet, brought face to face with a supply of threads, most people act as though this were still the case, when, in fact, today, the creative process is more useful in its own right, and, in our culture, is itself far more valuable to the individual than any of the materials that go into it.

Furthermore, if the aim is always merely to turn out something useful, there must necessarily be a tendency to take a familiar path, and a consequent reluctance to experiment. Therefore, while the final goal may indeed often be to make something, part of the time tatting and other handcrafts ought to be viewed as activities that are pursued for their own sake, either for relaxation or for the sense of well-being that results from the solution of fascinating though difficult problems. After all, there is no product when playing chess or cards,

and, unless a tape recorder is at hand, neither is there any tangible, lasting product when an orchestra plays a symphony.

In those instances where there is to be an end product, it should never be anything that attempts to compete with a more satisfactory machine-made item. For instance, in these days when the careful shopper can virtually eliminate ironing, it makes little sense to create things that need old-fashioned care, for instead of being used and enjoyed, they are sure to lie on a shelf or in a drawer, after being put to service only once or twice. Similarly, if the item one is thinking of making would be more serviceable if it were waterproof, and if a satisfactory manufactured version is available, it may be useless to try to make an equally good object by hand. For, often, materials that can be had by the manufacturer who buys on a large scale are simply not available to the craftsman.

Hopefully, as time goes on, and, especially, as the American craft movement grows, the picture will change. We are promised that soon we will be able to take our handmade fabrics to a neighborhood store where they will be processed to make ironing unnecessary, and, already, the widespread interest in macramé has brought new threads to the market. For the professional craftsman, some aspects of the problem must always remain, since his role is to point the way to the

8/A Neat Package

Finishing, Mounting, and Making Things

general public and to industry, and, in order to do so, he must constantly be on the lookout for new materials, some of which may be very hard to obtain unless he is closely connected with industry or has entered with others into some sort of large-scale buying group.

In the meanwhile, in spite of these limitations, there are many individual, serviceable, and beautiful objects that can be made that give much use and pleasure, and which, because they are unique, play a part in our lives that the machine-made object cannot fill. Wearing apparel that does not need frequent cleaning or that emerges from the dryer or comes down from the clothesline all ready to wear is well worth our time. Anything of highly durable and dirt-resistant materials that needs only to be wiped off occasionally with a cloth dampened with cleaning fluid or thick suds can give much useful service to the owner. Often, a fabric that would otherwise need constant care in the form of pressing becomes practical if it is stretched and mounted on a firm backing such as leather, fabric-covered buckram, or just another heavy fabric. It then falls into the category of things that can be cleaned with a damp cloth. Draperies and hangings, if they do not have breakable found objects incorporated into the design, and if they are not permanently attached to their

rods, may be put into the dryer and tossed without heat occasionally. It is amazing the amount of dust this removes and how long it puts off the day when any more drastic cleaning needs to be done. Hangings that will not go into the dryer may be vacuumed gently.

There are three products that are invaluable when finishing work that can help transform things into easy-care items. The first is a spray which makes fabrics soil-resistant and water-resistant. The second is fabric finish, which can be bought at the grocery. This is especially useful when a fabric is to be mounted. Applications should be made on the wrong side of the work, and up to three may be necessary. Care should be taken to keep the temperature of the iron low to prevent scorching. Experiment with different brands. Some seem to be easier to handle than others. The third item, which changes the character of any fabric drastically, is acrylic spray, which coats things with plastic. It should always be tested carefully on a small sample to see whether the change it makes will be satisfactory. It is relatively expensive, since, often, a great deal must be used to get the right effect. Dipping plastic for small items can also come in handy, as previously described in the section on earrings.

Ways to use tatting

For beginners, especially those who are timid about creating their own designs, good initial projects consist of anything that is based on a straight strip of one or more rows of tatting (fig. 8-2), or on a rectangle, square, or circle. Headbands, necklaces, bracelets, and placemats are all good. Fringed belts are currently popular, but if the result is to be satisfactory, the ends should be left quite long (too-short fringe is not at all decorative) and the fabric should be firm enough so that the belt will not twist into a nondescript rope when it is worn. If it starts to twist, it must be sewn to a backing.

Other projects that require only simple techniques and a minimum of finishing are small, rectangular wall hangings, pillow covers, and bags of various sorts (fig. 8-3). If bags or pillows are lined, ends can be conveniently hidden (fig. 8-4). See pages 46 and 69 for other suggestions about how to deal with the problem of ends

Garments. You can find many simple, easy-fitting garments in sewing instruction books that are nothing more than flat geometric shapes or tubes, such as ponchos, wrap-around skirts, shirts, and dresses. Admittedly, people with problem figures are not able to wear many of them, but this is less true than it used to be, and for most, they are just the thing for showing off highly decorative fabrics.

Furthermore, because tatting can be *shaped* by making successive rows longer or shorter than previous ones, clothing can be designed with the aid of modern shaped patterns (fig. 8-5). In general, though, it is best to avoid those that include darts.

Directions for drafting simple patterns to one's own measurements, such as are found in some knitting and weaving books (see Bibliography), are ideal, especially since tatting, too, is somewhat elastic. Remember that tatted garments can be planned so that all joining is done as the work progresses. There is seldom need to sew pieces together afterwards. If the project does call for sewing pieces of tatting together, it can be done very simply and invisibly with a matching sewing thread worked through convenient openings at the edges.

Figure 8-2. Belt with sequins. Although attachments can present complex tatting problems (see Chapter 7), simple belts can be constructed from a few rows of tatting, and fastened, as here, with a tatted chain loop and a button. (Courtesy of Dorothy Tooker.)

Figure 8-3. Round purse with sequins. A simple method of construction is demonstrated: two circles of tatting were created by working in larger and larger concentric rounds. Then they were joined at the edges, leaving a space for a zipper. The handle is attached to the zipper pull. (Courtesy of Dorothy Tooker.)

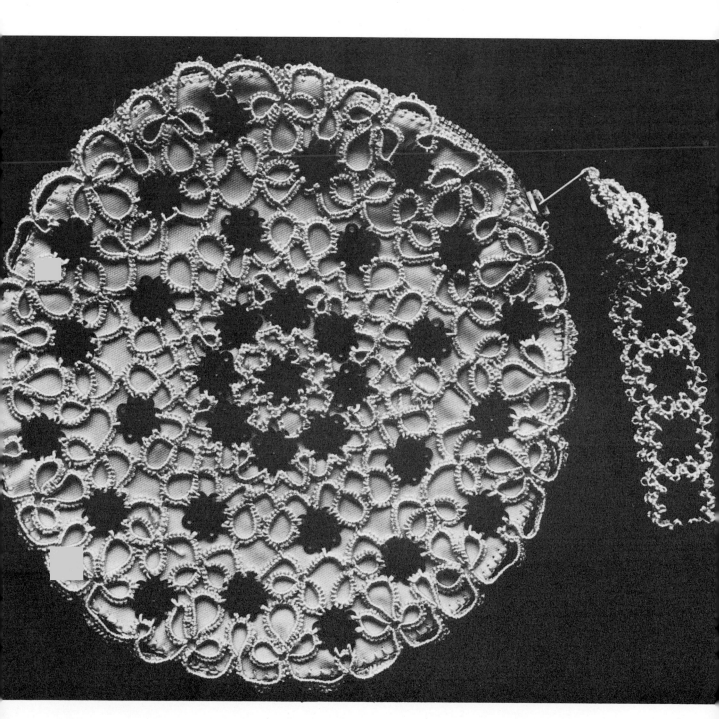

Figure 8-4. Another round purse, constructed in the same general way, of pearl cotton. The rosette in the center is created from overlapping chains. (Courtesy of Susan E. Munstedt. In the author's collection.)

Figure 8-5. The designer models her tatted vest of split polypropylene knitting yarn. (Courtesy of Susan E. Munstedt.)

Tatting as appliqué. Appliqué, a craft in itself, is also a very satisfactory way to decorate items with tatting. Even pieces that must be washed or cleaned often can be created this way, provided three precautions are observed. First, the thread that is used for the tatting must wash or dry clean in the same manner as the material to which it is sewn. Second, both appliqué and background must shrink at the same rate. Preshrink both if necessary before sewing them together. Third, the appliqué must be applied so that all parts of it will remain flat. In other words, it cannot merely be tacked down in the middle, but must be sewn down at very close intervals all around the edges (fig. 8-6). If there are picots, each one must be tacked down.

Tatting used as appliqué in panels on bags, pillows, backed hangings, and other objects allows the use of unconventional methods that would be impossible were there no supporting backing. For instance, very long picots can be made which can then be cut and twisted, and threads can be frayed and glued down where desired. Elgiva Nicholls has covered this subject thoroughly in her book, *A New Look in Tatting*.

Figure 8-6. Sewing down a tatted appliqué.

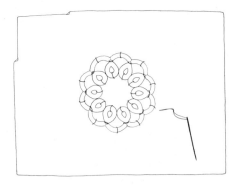

Trimmings and Inserts. Where it is used for trimming, as was so commonly done in the old days on handkerchiefs and domestic linens, tatting must also wash and shrink in the same fashion as the fabric it is applied to. A good trick to remember is that edging applied like braid, so that it does not hang free, is sure to lie flat after it is washed.

Inserts of tatted medallions can be applied to material that does not fray very readily, such as closely woven cotton or linen. Other material can sometimes be made less liable to fraying by treating the cut edges with modern iron-on adhesives, but first efforts at inserting should be done on the sturdier materials.

The piece to be cut out of the background fabric will be some geometric shape, such as a square, circle, oval, or triangle. Determine where the finished edges of this shape will lie by pinning the tatting in position on the background and then outlining the shape with small running stitches. Next, tack the tatting permanently to the background only through each edging picot or stitch that touches the line of running stitches. Turn the work over, and, from behind, cut out a hole, leaving a narrow allowance for turning under a hem. Clip this hem allowance right down to the stitching as shown for circular or square medallions in Figure 8-7. Clip into all the corners for angular shapes, and at frequent intervals around curved shapes. After clipping, turn back the edges, and hem, buttonhole, or otherwise finish them.

Once largely used for linens, this method has possible wide application for many objects, especially those where a see-through effect is wanted, as in a screen or window shade, or when a colorful lining fabric can show through to advantage. Inserted motifs are particularly attractive when combined with various kinds of surface embroidery.

Tatting can also be used to join two pieces of fabric as in Figure 8-9. The tatting serves both as a trimming and as an insert, in this case.

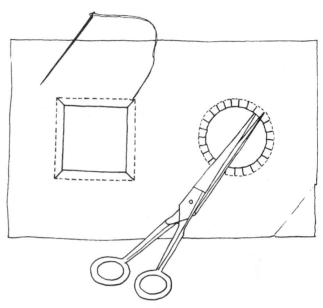

Figure 8-7. Preparing the background fabric for circular and square tatted inserts. First tack the tatting to the right side of fabric. The reverse of the fabric is shown here, with clipped curve in the circular insert.

Figure 8-8. Inserts were once widely used on domestic fabrics. Piano scarf, 1900–1910, with an insert reminiscent of Irish tatting. (Courtesy of Horner Museum, Oregon State University.)

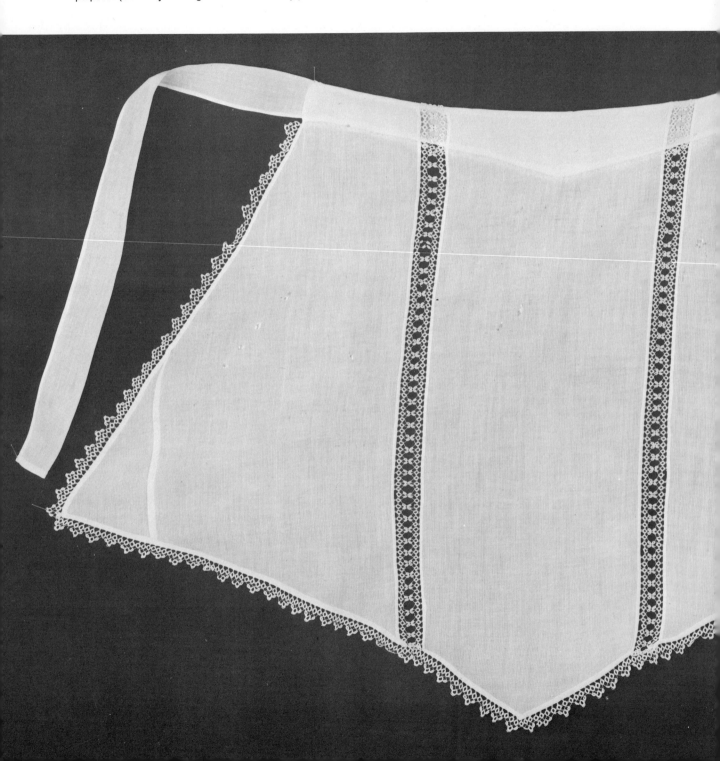

Figure 8-9. Apron with tatted insertions and edging, about 1910? Familiar tatting designs serve both a decorative and useful purpose. (Courtesy of Oregon Historical Society.)

Figure 8-10. Letter paper decorated with tatting and small leaves. (Courtesy of Lynda Ford Voris.)

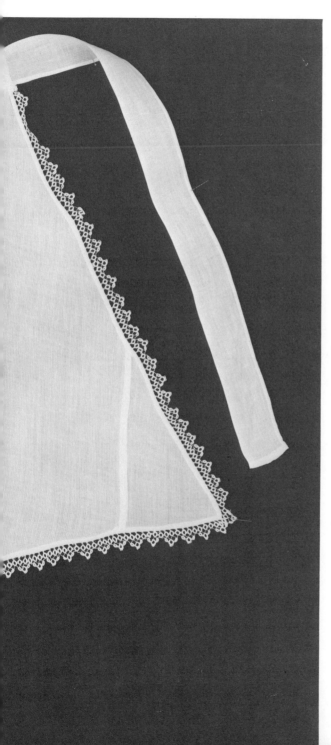

Just for fun. A great variety of quick projects can be made from single tatted motifs. Many people today like to make small tatted motifs of size 70 cotton and glue them to writing paper as decoration. Often, painted or inked embellishments are added. Larger, heavier bits of tatting can be used to decorate bulletin boards, etc. Even a belt, purse, or hair clip can be ornamented in this way.

Mounting hangings on dowels

Of all the varied and imaginative ways to mount hangings, using wooden dowels seems to be the most consistently popular. The dowels are inexpensive and easy to cut to size, and can be stained or painted at home. Tatting, like many other fabric techniques, creates loops, openings, and ends that can be used to attach the piece to the dowel.

Particularly attractive finials for tatted or other hangings can be made by covering wooden dowels with tatting (figs. 8-11, 8-12, and 8-13). Before starting the covering, drill holes in the dowels where required loops or ends will be attached. And, because it is easier to do the tatting before attaching the hanging, put doubled threads or cords through the holes to keep track of them and to provide an easy means of pulling the threads of the hanging through, when the covering is finished (figs. 8-14 and 8-15). Lay one end of the tatting thread along the dowel so that it will be covered as the work progresses. A bit of glue will secure the first half hitch or two. When the wood is covered, pull the end of the thread into a tapestry needle. Just next to the last knot, glue the thread lightly for a short distance, and quickly, before it has time to dry, pull the needle through the last two or three half hitches. After the glue dries, the thread will hold and may be cut close. Color the ends of the dowel with a felt-tipped marker to match the thread. Once the hanging has been mounted on the dowels, the ends can be arranged and secured in any way desired.

It might be a good idea to say, in passing, that while there are many pieces of hardware on the market to help in the finishing and mounting of handwork, some of it is of very poor quality, poor design, or both, and can detract greatly from the appearance of the finished product. This is especially true of jewelry findings. With a little thought, better mountings can usually be devised, frequently with the materials used for the object. A necklace, a purse, or a belt, for example, can be closed by means of a tatted ring and a bead or button.

Figures 8-11 and 8-12. Details of top and bottom of wall hanging of cotton cable twist. The finials, dowels in this case, are covered with tatting. After the ends of the hanging are pulled through, they can be crossed inconspicuously and glued.

Figure 8-13. Detail of bottom of wall hanging with ends pulled through a wooden bead. The top is shown in Figure 4-10.

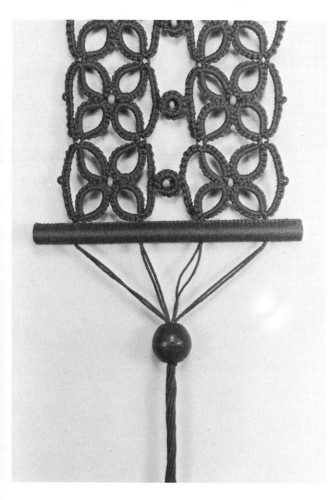

Figure 8-14. Covering the dowel with tatting to make a finial for a hanging.

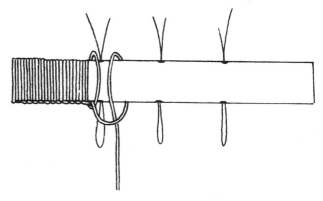

Figure 8-15. Pulling the ends of the tatted hanging through the holes in the dowel.

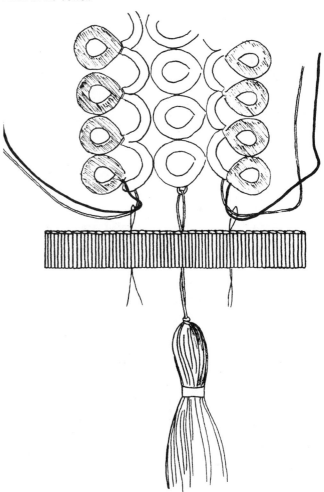

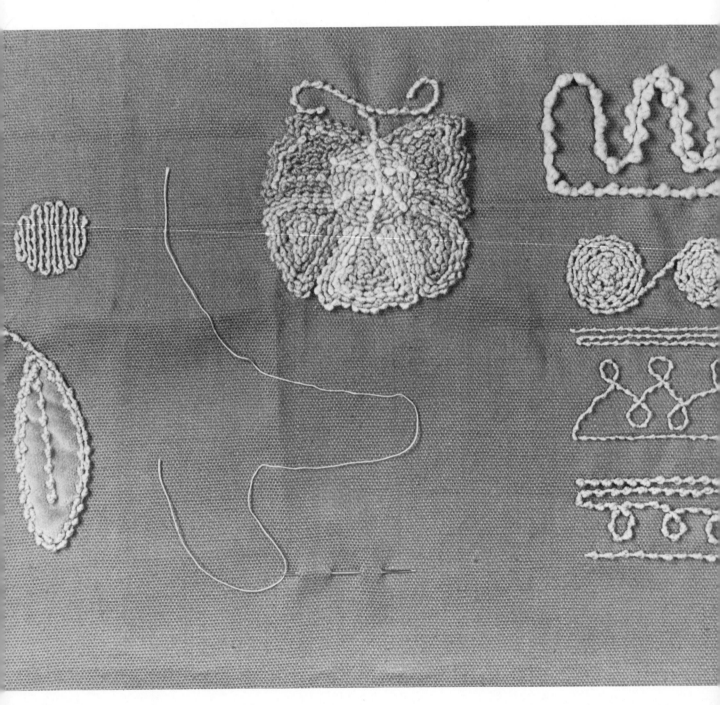

Figure 9-1. Sampler of couched knotting reflecting a traditional approach. Various kinds of threads are used, but only one knot (see fig. 9-3 c), which was often used in the eighteenth century.

9/The Full Circle

Contemporary Knotting

Obsolete and obscure, the seventeenth and eighteenth century embroidery technique of couched knotting has been completely overlooked by today's craftsmen. But it can contribute much to both embroidery and tatting, for it stands as a technical transition, as well as a historical link, between the two.

Couched knotting, or knotted-line embroidery (fig. 9-1), is formed from a series of knots that are tacked down to the background fabric in various places. The knots provide a rich textural interest to the stitchery, and could be most striking if done in heavy contemporary materials. Knotting is simple and interesting enough to serve as an introduction for children and adults to both embroidery and tatting, yet it has many variations and lends itself well to modern ideas. The simplest knots resemble knotted embroidery stitches, and the complex ones approach the form of the tatted ring.

The pictures in this chapter show various forms of knotting, without, by any means, exhausting the possibilities. In every case, you must make a ring with the same hand position as in tatting, put one or more knots on it, changing the knot-bearer of course, close the ring, and repeat the process. After the

first ring is closed, attempt to make the second and all succeeding ones right up close to the previous knot, and the knots will space themselves quite evenly.

The knots on a single thread or cord may be all the same kind, as in the photographs, or they may be varied, which can produce visually exciting patterns and textures. Tatting forms can most easily be combined with the knotting, as was probably done in the past. Mrs. Delany, whose chair covers show a transition between knotting and tatting (see page 13) used a kind of knotting called *sugar plum* in which the central leaf of a triple cluster appears to be a tatted ring, and the smaller ones Josephine knots.

For more contemporary work, other kinds of knots may be used as well, and there is always the possibility of putting a needle on the same thread and continuing with embroidery, tapestry, needlepoint, or needlepoint-lace stitches. The combinations are waiting to be explored — it is an open field for experimentation. Knotting, like tatting, can be combined with many kinds of threadwork: crochet, hairpin lace, weaving (see fig. 6-14) and embroidery (see figs. 6-16 and 6-17). The wrapped and tatted necklace in Figure 6-10 suggests how macramé might be used.

Figure 9-2. Fragment of a doily made with a "tatting hook" by Yvonne Saint-Pierre in French Canada in 1910. Although described as crochet, this piece appears to have many knots. (Courtesy of National Museums of Canada.)

Figure 9-3. Several kinds of knotting, including a line with short loops. Included are French stitch (a), a double form of French stitch (b), double tatting knot (c), triple half knots (d), bullion knots (e), two double tatting knots separated by a long picot (f).

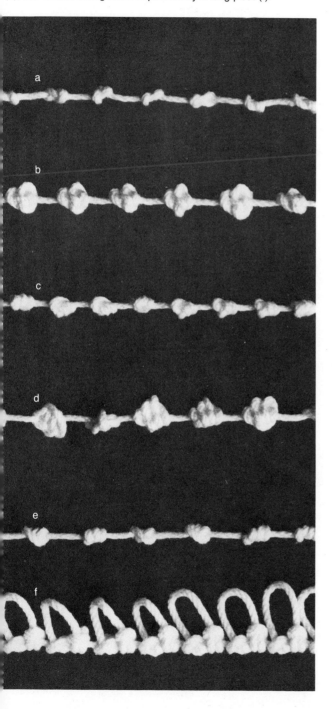

Figure 9-3 shows a progression of knots from very simple to complex. In *a*, each ring contains only the first half of the tatting knot. This is the knotting equivalent of tatting's French stitch. In *b*, again only the first half of the knot is used, but this time two are made. The rings in *c* each contain one double tatting knot. Many people, when they see this pattern couched down, will recognize it as something that often decorated eighteenth-century waistcoats.

Couching is a popular embroidery technique in which a thread, or several threads placed together, are sewn down with another thread. Originally this was a technique for securing threads which were too heavy or too stiff to be taken through the background fabric in the usual way, and so they were whipped down, more or less invisibly, with fine matching sewing thread. In contemporary work, heavy contrasting threads are often used to do the the sewing, thus achieving an even more decorative effect, and, instead of whipping, various embroidery stitches like fly stitch, detached chain stitch, buttonhole stitch, and blocks of satin stitch are worked over the cords. The material being couched down can be laid in a straight line, twisted to form curves, etc., and even laid across itself, perhaps in a trellis. Some of the historical photographs (see figs. 1-4 and 1-5) show what kinds of dense patterns and shapes can be achieved when closely-knotted thread is couched down invisibly after the knotting is completed, using small, nearly invisible, whipping stitches between every knot. With heavier cord or yarn, a few lines of spaced knotting could be very effective, and using embroidery stitches widens the possibilities even further. Any article that will get much wear, and especially those that will have to be laundered, must have very close couching or the knotting will pull loose and twist.

The rings in Fig. 9-3d each have three half knots. Any of the composite knots above can be varied by making them out of a greater number of individual knots before closing the ring.

The bullion knots shown in *e* are made by throwing the shuttle over the ring thread three times (fig. 9-5). These can be elongated by making more windings. The belt in Figure 4-9 uses such knots to advantage.

Knotting, like tatting, also uses loops and picots. In Figure 9-3f, each knot contains two double tatting knots separated by a large picot. The design would be effective used as braided edgings are. Figure 9-6 is really the same stitch, used as a kind of fringe. Each ring contains two double

Figure 9-4. Detail of contemporary panel of spider and web. Tatted chains of various thicknesses were couched down to the background, and tiny transparent beads sewn on, all in one operation. (Courtesy of Lynda Ford Voris.)

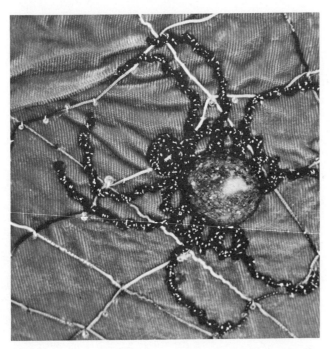

stitches, a very long picot, and two more double stitches. In the process of couching, this fringe can be cut, twisted, frayed, or knotted further.

Figure 9-7 is a series of complex knots ending with tatted rings. The Josephine picots in *a* consist of six half stitches each. They may also be drawn up into lumps to make Josephine knots (see fig. 5-2b).

The small rings in *b* are drawn up only enough to form half circles. To make them: r, 2ds, 3 p sep by lds, 2ds, cl. The row of tatted rings in *c* is joined by the picots at the sides of each ring. Rings which are not attached to each other could be couched alternately one up and one down. Triple clusters can also be used, especially if the center one is large and the other two small, as in Mrs. Delaney's sugar plums, which had a trefoil shape.

And so we have come the full circle from knotting to tatting back to knotting again. This chapter clearly shows the relationship between the two and how one developed into the other.

Figure 9-6. Very long loops can add variety to knotting.

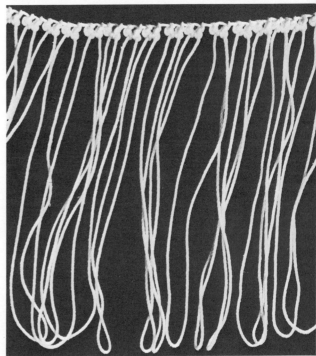

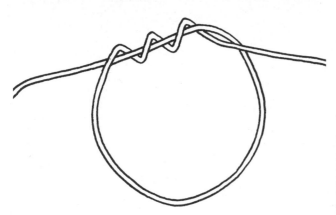

Figure 9-5. Making a bullion knot.

Figure 9-7. Tatted rings and half rings can also be used in knotting, combined with simpler forms or alone. Included are Josephine picots (a), half-closed rings (b), and tatted rings joined at side picots (c).

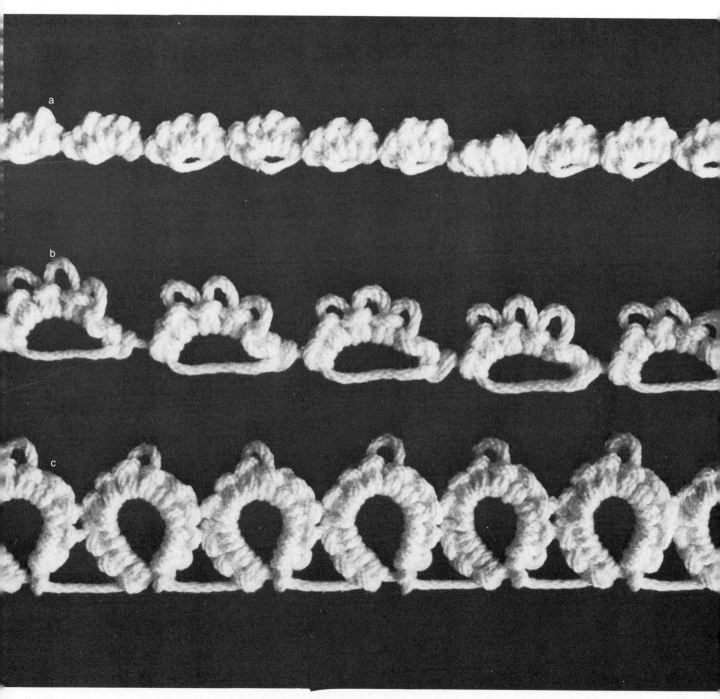

Bibliography

Anchor Manual of Needlework. 3d ed. Newton Center, Mass.: Branford, 1968. Good, traditional tatting designs in a fascinating book on embroidery and lace techniques, many of which are hard to find elsewhere.

Ashdown, Elsie A. *Tatting,* Craft Notebook Series, no. 9. London: Mills & Boon, 1961. An excellent brief introduction to tatting techniques.

Attenborough, Bessie M. *The Craft of Tatting*. Newton Center, Mass.: Branford, 1972. ". . . this work features patterns which can be found in the tatting chapter of most books on needlecraft techniques." — Lois Horowitz in the *Library Journal* (March 1, 1973).

Blomqvist, Gun, and Persson, Elwy. *Frivoliteter* [Tatting]. Stockholm: LTs Förlag, 1967. In Swedish. English translation to be published by Van Nostrand Reinhold.

Caulfeild, Sophia F. A., and Saward, Blanche C. *The Dictionary of Needlework: An Encyclopaedia of Artistic, Plain and Fancy Needlework*. Facsimile of the 1882 edition. New York: Arno Press, distributed by Crown Publishers, 1972. Of historical interest, or for those who want to tat lappets from quaint directions. Do not overlook the section on crochet tatting.

Coats Sewing Group Books: *Time for Tatting,* no. 813; *Learn Tatting,* no. 1088; *Tatting,* no. 919. Glasgow: Coats Sewing Group, 1968–70. Traditional designs, more unusual than most, which suggest ideas for contemporary work.

De Dillmont, Thérèse. *Encyclopedia of Needlework,* DMC Library. Mulhouse, France: Editions Th. de Dillmont, n.d. This 1886 classic has a section on tatting, and an interesting one on Victorian needlework trimmings, including pompons and tassels.

Duncan, Ida Riley. *The Complete Book of Progressive Knitting*. 1940. Reprint. New York: Liveright, 1968. Includes information on drafting garment patterns from body measurements, a technique that can be adapted to tatting needs. Similar material is also covered in the same author's *Knit to Fit* (New York: Liveright, 1963).

Groves, Sylvia. *The History of Needlework Tools and Accessories*. [Feltham, Middlesex, England: Published for] Country Life Books [by Hamlyn Publishing Group], 1966. Chapter 10 is a short, but carefully-researched and accurate history of tatting.

Hartung, Rolf. *Creative Textile Design: Thread and Fabric*. New York: Reinhold Publishing Corp., 1963. A cursory reading of this ingenious little book yields nothing, but the reader who plays the game as outlined finds that the author has discovered a way to teach creative inventiveness.

Hoare, Katharine L. *The Art of Tatting,* with an introd. by H. M. the Queen of Roumania. London: Longmans, 1910. Chiefly photographs of the unique work of both these ladies. The Queen, also known as Carmen Sylva, used heavy threads and beads to turn out almost-contemporary work. Some of the author's tatting, applied to net grounds, resembled Alençon lace.

Krøncke, Grete. *Mounting Handicraft: Ideas and Instructions for Assembling and Finishing*. New York: Van Nostrand Reinhold Co., 1967. An excellent introductory manual, which, regrettably, omits pompons and tassels.

Macfarlan, Allan and Paulette. *Knotcraft: The Art of Knot Tying*. New York: Association Press, 1967. Includes some interesting background on the history of knots.

Newton, Stella Mary. "Mrs. Delany and Her Handiwork." *Antiques,* July 1969, pp. 100–5. Background on Mrs. Delany and her knotting. The article includes a photograph of one of her blue and white chair covers.

Nicholls, E[lgiva] A. *A New Look in Tatting: Flowers, Leaves and Picture Composition*. London: Alec Tiranti, 1959. The only book on tatting published so far in this century that offers new ideas!

Nicholls, Elgiva [A.]. *Tatting*. New York: Taplinger, 1962. A book on how to tat which also supplies descriptions of the contents of several nineteenth-century English pattern books, one as early as 1843.

[Ramos Folqués, María Rosa]. *Encaje de lanzaderas,* Creaciones alindae nos. 1-. Madrid: Distributed by Paraninfo (Meléndez Valdés, 65), n.d. In Spanish. Volume 2 has diagrams as well as instructions and photographs.

Rosenberg, Sharon, and Wiener, Joan. *The Illustrated Hassle-Free Make Your Own Clothes Book*. New York: Bantam Books, 1971. Directions for drafting simple clothing patterns (belts, bags and pillows as well) that can be used to plan tatted garments.

Severn, Bill. *Rope Roundup: The Lore and Craft of Rope and Roping*. Illus. by Yukio Tashiro. New York: David McKay, 1960. Includes much information about knot records as well as basic knots and how to tie them.

Scott, Robert Gillam. *Design Fundamentals*. New York: McGraw-Hill Book Co., 1951. A good place to begin the lifelong study of design that is essential if one expects to do more than pedestrian work in the handcrafts.

Tatting, DMC Library. New ed. Mulhouse, France: DMC, 1968. A slightly-changed version of the pattern book formerly published by the now-defunct Cartier-Bresson thread company. Beautiful, simple designs!

Thaler, Lora. *No Pattern Sewing,* Dell Purse Book 6377. [New York]: Dell Publishing Co., 1972. More simple pattern drafting in a very inexpensive booklet often to be found on the local newsstand.

Thomas, Mary. *Mary Thomas's Book of Knitting Patterns*. London: Hodder and Stoughton, 1943. In addition to a brief discussion on how to draft modern garments from measurements, this book also includes a section on seamless peasant garments.

Patterns for Tatting, p-490, 1970; *Tatting Notes,* p-480, 1970. Tower Press, 25 Garden Street, Danvers, Mass. 01923. Inexpensive pamphlets which feature tatting in the traditional manner.

Wardle, Patricia. *Victorian Lace*. New York: Praeger, 1969. Includes a detailed discussion of the tatting industry in nineteenth-century Ireland.

Wilson, Jean. *Weaving You Can Wear*. New York: Van Nostrand Reinhold, 1973. Contains instructions for pattern drafting of many simply constructed garments.

Suppliers and Manufacturers

UNITED STATES

If you cannot find these product lines in your local stores, write to the manufacturers for a list of distributors.

The Boye Needle Company
4343 N. Ravenswood Avenue
Chicago, Illinois 60613/Manufacturer of red plastic tatting shuttle.

The DMC Corporation
107 Trumbull Street
Elizabeth, New Jersey 07206/Manufacturer of first-rate line of 6-cord mercerized crochet cotton, including size 3.

Frederick J. Fawcett, Inc.
129 South Street
Boston, Massachusetts 02111/Manufacturer and supplier of all kinds of linen thread.

Knit Services, Inc.
3001 Indianola Avenue
Columbus, Ohio 43202/Supplier of cotton and nylon macramé cords (many of which are also suitable for tatting) nylon stitching twine, and Lily's Double-Quick.

Lily Mills Company
Shelby, North Carolina 28150/Manufacturer and supplier of cotton cable twist (Double-Quick), polypropylene macramé cord, satin cord, and many other threads suitable for tatting.

Merribee Needlecraft Company
2904 West Lancaster
Fort Worth, Texas 76107/Mail-order house with retail outlets in several cities across the country. Has full line of DMC 6-cord, including size 3, and shuttles suitable for fine tatting.

Phentex USA, Inc.
P.O. Box 99
Plattsburgh, New York, 12901/Distributors of polypropylene knitting yarn.

Robin and Russ Handweavers
533 North Adams Street
McMinnville, Oregon 97128/Weaver's supply house that carries a full line of threads, including nylon stitching twine, macramé cord, cotton cable twist, satin cord, rami, and linen threads.

Yarn Center
866 Avenue of the Americas
New York, New York/Retailer carrying many lines of cotton macramé and crocheting cords, including DMC.

CANADA

Handcraft House
56 Esplanade
North Vancouver, British Columbia

Village Weaver
551 Church Street
Toronto, Ontario

Mrs. E. Blackburn
R. R. #2
Caledon East, Ontario

UNITED KINGDOM

For all kinds of ropes, strings, nylon cords, fine twines, etc.

M. Mallock and Sons
44 Vauxhall Bridge Road
London SW1

Arthur Beale
194 Shaftesbury Avenue
London WC2 (Both sell over the counter to the general public and will sell small quantities.)

British Twines Ltd.
112 Green Lanes
London N16 (For schools or colleges who order in quantity, British Twines will dye strings to specification. Also, there are at times oddments of coloured strings at the factory, which they will sell off.)

Dryad Ltd
Northgates
Leicester, LE1 40R (Dryads sell a fine natural macramé twine in half-pound balls, but will only accept orders by post of the minimum value of £ 2.)

The Hobby Horse
15–17 Langton Street
London SW8

For piping cord and a variety of other yarns

(In boxes, containing 23m (25 yards) of the thickest cord to 274m (300 yards) of the finest: bought this way, piping cord works out very economically.)

McCulloch and Wallis Ltd.
25–26 Dering Street
London W1

For rug wools, knitting wools, embroidery threads, nylon cords, synthetic metal thread and shuttles

The Needlewoman Shop
146–148 Regent Street
London W1

For beads, if required

Ells and Farrier Ltd.
5 Princes Street
London W1

Bourne and Hollingsworth Ltd
Oxford Street
London W1

The Needlewoman Shop
146–148 Regent Street
London W1

Index

Abbreviations

ch	chain
cl	close
ds	double stitch, double stitches
p	picot, picots
r	ring
rw	reverse work
sep	separated
sp	space

Note: The direction *change shuttles* as used in this book refers to the shuttle or its substitute.